THE TREASURED WOMAN

THE TREASURED WOMAN

PROFILES FROM PROVERBS 31

CHRISTA BRYANT

ISBN-10: 1941972551
ISBN-13: 978-1941972557

Library of Congress Control Number: 2015933262

Published by Start2Finish Books
PO Box 680, Bowie, Texas 76230
www.start2finish.org

Printed in the United States of America

Cover Design: Josh Feit, Evangela.com

For Dewayne

My heart trusts in you.

TABLE OF CONTENTS

1.	The Proverbs 31 Woman	9
2.	Mary, Mother of Jesus	19
3.	Mary & Martha	27
4.	Priscilla, Lois, & Eunice	35
5.	Tabitha	42
6.	Ruth, Naomi's Daughter-in-Law	49
7.	Ruth, Boaz's Wife	56
8.	Abigail	63
9.	Deborah	71
10.	Rahab	78
11.	Hannah	85
12.	Esther	92
13.	The 21st Century Woman	100

An excellent wife who can find?
    She is far more precious than jewels.
The heart of her husband trusts in her,
    and he will have no lack of gain.
She does him good, and not harm,
    all the days of her life.
She seeks wool and flax,
    and works with willing hands.
She is like the ships of the merchant;
    she brings her food from afar.
She rises while it is yet night
    and provides food for her household
    and portions for her maidens.
She considers a field and buys it;
    with the fruit of her hands she plants a vineyard.
She dresses herself with strength
    and makes her arms strong.
She perceives that her merchandise is profitable.
    Her lamp does not go out at night.
She puts her hands to the distaff,
    and her hands hold the spindle.
She opens her hand to the poor
    and reaches out her hands to the needy.
She is not afraid of snow for her household,
    for all her household are clothed in scarlet.
She makes bed coverings for herself;
    her clothing is fine linen and purple.
Her husband is known in the gates
    when he sits among the elders of the land.
She makes linen garments and sells them;
    she delivers sashes to the merchant.
Strength and dignity are her clothing,
    and she laughs at the time to come.

She opens her mouth with wisdom,
and the teaching of kindness is on her tongue.
She looks well to the ways of her household
and does not eat the bread of idleness.
Her children rise up and call her blessed;
her husband also, and he praises her:
"Many women have done excellently,
but you surpass them all."
Charm is deceitful, and beauty is vain,
but a woman who fears the LORD is to be praised.
Give her of the fruit of her hands,
and let her works praise her in the gates.

— Prov. 31:10-31

1

THE PROVERBS 31 WOMAN

PROVERBS 31:10-31

She is far more precious than jewels. — Prov. 31:10

Christina Rossetti wrote in one of her famous poems, "Who has seen the wind? Neither I nor you: But when the leaves hang trembling The wind is passing through." None of us have ever seen the Proverbs 31 woman, yet we have all trembled at the effect she has had on our lives. Unfortunately, instead of seeing the Proverbs 31 woman for who she is in Scripture, we see the ideal woman perpetuated by our culture. To some, she is a superhero or Wonder Woman. She has the perfect family, the perfect marriage, and the perfect reputation, all nestled into the perfect home. To others, she is the antithesis of the feminine movement. She is a symbol of weakness under the overbearing rule of her husband. And yet, to others, she is simply an imaginary woman, a literary device or a nice thought written into Proverbs with nothing relevant to contribute to how a 21st-century woman should conduct herself. In Scripture, however, she is a woman of virtue and noble character, one who was taken seriously by the people of Israel. She was admired and respected. She was a woman fit to be queen. She was a woman inspired by God.

Even though the treasured woman of Proverbs 31 was not an actual woman, her qualities are reflected in the lives of the women of Israel. Each woman mentioned in the Bible is there for a reason. Her decisions and actions made a difference in the lives of the Israelites or impacted the future of Christianity. However, for all of the honor bestowed upon these women in Scripture, they are also a lot like us. They faced trials and temptations similar to ours. They desired love and accomplishment. They were sinners and doubters. So what has set them apart? How did their stories end up in the Bible? It's because they feared the Lord. They are the Proverbs 31 woman.

Fear of the Lord can cause women just like us to overcome our doubts and insecurities in order to do great things for him just like the women of the Bible. That respect also drives us to be like the Proverbs 31 woman—the epitome of treasured womanhood. God made womanhood to be a beautiful, captivating part of his creation. Just as the women of Scripture showed the excellent nature of the Father in heaven by aspiring to be the woman God envisioned, we too can proclaim his excellencies by becoming a Proverbs 31 woman.

THE POETRY OF PROVERBS 31

By inspiration, King Lemuel, perhaps a symbolic name for King Solomon, penned Proverbs 31. Perhaps he was recording the advice of his mother or a common poem of the day. Some people believe it was a poem written by Abraham for his beloved Sarah. No one is quite sure. However, the poem was beloved by the Israelites and recited by young Hebrew women for centuries at their Sabbath-day feasts. We do know that the passage details the kind of wife the king of Israel should choose—the kind of woman God wanted as queen.

We must also consider the possibility that the passage was written by King Lemuel's mother, quite possibly Bathsheba and a queen herself. If the passage had been written by a woman in a position of royalty, then we must also assume that the many attributes listed in Proverbs 31 are not just desired by God, but also attainable by women. These attributes were not only obtainable in the days of King Lemuel but also today. God has set before us a pattern we can follow so that we can more closely align ourselves to the woman God wants us to become.

Thankfully, we have this blueprint outlining the woman God wants us to be. However, with that blueprint comes great responsibility that can also foster great doubt. As we look at this woman, consider all she does, and compare her life to ours, we may feel inadequate. Few of us consider fields and buy them. Few of us plant vineyards or make all of our family's clothing. So we must ask ourselves, in an age of the Internet and thirty-minute meals, how can the Proverbs 31 woman influence us? What was it about her that made her virtuous and noble in character?

And can I ever be such a treasured woman as her?

If we are to striving to be the woman described in Proverbs 31, we must first take apart the passage, find the characteristics that make up who she is, and seek to apply them to our daily lives whether as wives, daughters, or servants of the King. Only by finding the underlying qualities the virtuous woman had in ancient times can we adapt them to the modern world. However, as much as the domesticity of the ancient world has morphed into the managing of a 21st-century household, little has changed about who a woman is and how God sees her. The virtuous woman of Scripture can be the treasured woman of today.

The passage in Prov. 31:10-31 is what Hebrew scholars call a chiasmus. This type of poetry was one in which the first ten lines begin with the first ten letters of the Hebrew alphabet. The second ten lines are the same ten letters written in reverse. Each line corresponds to its matching letter (see below). For instance, v. 10 corresponds with v. 30, v. 13 corresponds with verse 27, etc. The middle of the poem is v. 23. This is the central thought of the poem and the ultimate discerning characteristic of the Proverbs 31 woman. That verse simply says, "Her husband is known in the gates when he sits among the elders of the land."

A.__________

B.________

C.______

D.

C'.______

B'.________

A'.__________

As King Lemuel was writing this passage, he was describing the best of what he was looking for in a wife and what we now know as the virtuous woman, the wife of noble character, or the treasured woman. However, the passage's main point seems to be a little anticlimactic, describing a man instead of a woman. In fact, saying her husband sits at the main gates seems like a criticism of this woman who works so hard and has earned a stellar reputation.

Quite the opposite, however! This line is the ultimate compliment for her. By saying her husband sits at the main gates, the writer is emphasizing that her husband is well-known and respected. For him to be so well-respected must mean his wife brings him honor and admiration. Her very life is one reason he is held in such high esteem. He values her and her reputation beyond the most expensive treasure!

As women, we all want that kind of appreciation and devotion from our husbands. We all want him to be proud of us publicly and know we bring him great blessings. How much more should we desire that relationship with God? To know that our very lives bring our Father both honor and glory and cause him to be respected at the "gates"—this should be our ultimate goal. Everything in our lives should glorify God and point to his love. The apostle Peter states, "But you are a chosen race, a royal priesthood, a holy nation, a people for his own possession, that you may proclaim the excellencies of him who called you out of darkness into his marvelous light" (1 Pet. 2:9). By her actions and demeanor, the treasured woman of Proverbs 31 proclaims the excellencies of the Father, bringing him praise and glory and honor. Many women in the Bible did this, and so can we.

WHAT MAKES HER SO VALUABLE?

We as readers can be struck with a sense of awe at what makes up this ideal woman, and we can struggle to find a place in our lives where we can relate to such high standards. None of us are perfect, nor will any of us become the queen of Israel. But the qualities she upholds can be demonstrated in grand palaces, poor, tiny hovels, or the most demanding of all places: suburban America. Fortunately, God did not allow us simply to guess at what those qualities are or how to go about developing them in our lives. He endowed them in real women, in real and difficult situations, and recorded them for us in Scripture so that we could learn from them and ultimately become the woman God intended us to be.

The women of Scripture probably had very different lifestyles than we do today, but many of their struggles are the same as ours. They wanted safe, caring homes. They wanted children and respect. They wanted loving, devoted husbands, and they wanted to be servants of the Lord. The trials that brought these women hope and redemption are similar to our own: Hannah endured teasing and bullying by Peninnah because of her barrenness; Rahab overcame a sullied reputation as a prostitute, Ruth grieved and took risks, and Esther faced personal peril by approaching the king and speaking out and up for Israel. These women all share similarities with the Proverbs 31 woman as they endured and overcame the challenges they faced. God blessed each of them mightily for conquering their fears and remaining faithful to him.

The Proverbs 31 woman has many attributes that we should cultivate. By reading the passage, we see that she is a woman who did not put herself first, but discovered her talents, abilities, and qualities and used them to serve God, her husband, her children, her servants, and the poor. Each activity had at the heart of its accomplishment her desire to help others and love God.

Showing God's love to those around us can influence others, but more importantly, by doing the righteous and good thing, we reflect God's holiness. The Proverbs 31 woman does this consistently. In v. 11, we see that she has established a relationship with her husband that makes trust and loyalty easy. Her husband trusts her in all that she does for their family. She did not earn this trust by being flattering or manipulative, but by working hard, choosing the family's welfare over her own, and always being honest with him in their dealings. In Scripture, we read about Mary who also earned the trust of the Lord and willingly accepted the task of bearing his Son.

In v. 13, the treasured woman works with willing hands. Doing this while serving others is not always easy to do. Doing laundry or purchasing clothes for our family may seem like a chore. If we complain every time we fold a towel or tackle the growing laundry pile, we have not worked with willing hands. How are we to glorify God if we complain while doing his work? And even more laborious for us may be teaching a Bible class or visiting the sick, but she, the treasured woman of Proverbs 31, does it willingly. Her love for the people around her was greater than her fears. In the book of Ruth, we see one of the hardest working women of the Bible. She loved and respected Naomi so much that she was willing to work for her even without reward. She did not have to help Naomi, but Ruth worked with willing hands.

In v. 14, she brings food from afar for her family. She has thought about what to feed her household and sought to accomplish those plans. Her desire to give her family the best is not just bragging rights; it is making sure her family knows they have received her best.

In v. 16, she considers a field and buys it. She has put a great deal of thought into the decisions she makes. She saves for her purchases, and she considers whether those purchases will be a good buy for her husband and family. No decision, important or trivial, can be made without considering the effects on our family, our relationships, and our faith. By carefully considering each choice, her family knows, and God knows, that it was made with the best of intentions. Mary and Martha were also given a choice when Jesus came to their house. They could take the time to listen to Jesus, or they could go about their lives. Mary considered her options and chose the Lord.

In v. 17, the Proverbs 31 woman dresses herself with strength and dignity. Those who look upon her know she is someone that should be respected, and she has not been weakened by the trials of life. More often than not, our appearance is a direct reflection of our heart and mindset. If we want the world to know we are strong in character, we must present ourselves in a way that reflects that characteristic. Abigail, during a moment of great trial, presented herself to David with strength, dignity, and humility. If Abigail can take on risk to her own life, so can we.

In v. 18, her lamp does not go out at night. She is committed to her family and their needs regardless of the hour. Her family knows they can come to her, and she is prepared to meet their needs. She is ready for that late-night call for help.

In v. 20, her hand reaches out to the poor. She takes time to think about them, their needs, and finds ways to provide for them. In our culture, those in poverty are usually an afterthought, receiving our leftovers—the things we were going to throw out anyway. The Proverbs 31 woman, however, plans for the poor. She considers them just as she does her family and makes provisions for them as she goes about her daily tasks. In the Bible, we read about Tabitha, a woman who spent her time making beautiful garments for those less fortunate. She honored them with her work and did not just give them her cast-off scraps.

In v. 21, we read that she is not afraid of snow because her family is well provided. She is prepared for whatever may come in inclement weather. It takes great faith not to worry about what will come. In an age when winter coats are plentiful, long underwear abounds, and wooly socks line the department stores, we tend to worry more about how warm our children will be. But she was not afraid. She knew the task was complete, and she set aside her fears. Unfortunately in today's world, we cannot always be prepared for the spiritual chill that may envelop our family. No wooly socks can prevent the trauma of being unprepared to deal with the storms of life.

In v. 27, she looks well to the ways of her household. Rahab looked well to the ways of her household. She chose a foreign God over the gods of Jericho, because she knew the Lord would protect her.

In v. 26, the teaching of kindness is on her tongue. She is a woman who is not rude and does not gossip. She is one from whom others can learn, because she always speaks with kindness and guidance. She thinks before she opens her mouth.

In v. 30, we see that she loves the Lord, and she loves the spiritual above the physical. Beyond all the things the world has to offer, she knows her commitment and loyalty to the Lord are what truly matter. Everything she does is not just a reflection of herself and her husband, but her Creator. Her fear of God is worthy of praise. As the queen of Persia, Esther had the world at her fingertips. She could have valued the things she had been given or the power she had. Instead, her fear of the Lord was greater. Her obedience saved the nation of Israel.

While these qualities and works of the Proverbs 31 woman may seem difficult to attain, the love and commitment she has for the Lord are not. As we read about the different women of Scripture, we will see that their love for the Lord is the common thread that binds them together. In the same way, love for the Lord is also the cord that binds together today's godly women. We can learn from the women of old, and we can encourage the women of today to be who God wants us to be. There is no greater joy than sitting with your fellow sisters in Christ praying, singing, and worshipping a powerful Savior. By putting Christ first, we have entered into that royal priesthood, and together we can proclaim the excellencies of the One who created us.

DISCUSSION QUESTIONS:

1. What is your first impression of the Proverbs 31 woman? How do you think society sees her?

2. Which of the qualities listed do you most admire? Why?

3. What are some qualities of the Proverbs 31 woman that you would like to adopt?

4. How could you make them fit into your lifestyle?

5. In light of the Proverbs 31 woman, which of your qualities could use some attention?

6. How can you increase those attributes in your life?

7. How could the virtues of Proverbs 31 woman apply to someone who is unmarried or who has no children?

8. What can you learn from modern-day Proverbs 31 women?

2

MARY, MOTHER OF JESUS

LUKE 1:26-37

The heart of her husband trusts in her. — Prov. 31:11

No matter your situation in life, being a parent is never easy. Suddenly you are responsible for the physical, spiritual, and emotional well-being of a tender, moldable soul. For Mary, being the mother of the Son of God must have seemed like an impossible task, especially to a young, unmarried, inexperienced woman. But that is what God called the young virgin Mary to be—the mother of his Son. As a wife, bearing a child for your husband is one of the greatest gifts you have the honor of giving. Being asked by God to bear his Son was an honor given to Mary that many in the world have chosen to worship. While that worship is not biblical, we can still admire, appreciate, and learn from the choices Mary made that fateful day when the angel Gabriel came to visit.

ENCOUNTERING GOD'S WILL

In Luke 1:26, we read about the encounter between Mary and Gabriel. Mary is quite taken back by the angel's words and fearful of what he has to say to her. However, Gabriel reassures Mary. He says in v. 30, "Do not be afraid, Mary, for you have found favor with God." Are those not the words we all long to hear from God—that we have found favor with him? Because the Lord had found favor with her and trusted her, he asked Mary to bear his child. Just as the woman in Proverbs 31 has built a relationship with her husband, Mary had shown faith and loyalty to God, and God knew her heart to be faithful to him. Because of her faith, God asked her to do an important task for the salvation of the world.

The task did not come easily. Mary was asked to endure the hardships of pregnancy during a time and in a place where little or no medical attention would be available to her. Her baby would not be born in a clean, comfortable hospital or a loving, warm home—but in a dank, dark cave. Doctors, nurses, or midwives would not be surrounding her; rather, an unsure husband and the uncaring stare of dirty animals would witness the birth of her baby. Her child would not be laid in a soft cradle made by loving hands, but in a stone trough in which animals had eaten and drooled. None of us would have chosen this place or situation for the birth of our baby. However, God led Mary there, and she willingly complied.

The physical conditions of Jesus' birth were dark and grim. But they cannot compare to the emotional conditions that would have plagued Mary during her pregnancy. The people of ancient Israel did not look kindly upon unwed mothers. Mary's condition would not have just caused stares and gossip, but would have essentially alienated her and her entire family from polite society. Joseph would have left Mary had the angels not visited him in Matt. 1:18.

However, Joseph could have done much more. He could have turned Mary in to the authorities as a loose woman and had her executed for her crimes. Her family could have been shunned. And while Mary had every reason to be joyous about carrying the Son of God in her womb, how many of her friends and family believed her about her virginity or that the angel Gabriel had visited her? How many of them would have shared her joy? How many of us today would have looked favorably upon Mary?

Mary could have said no. She could have told the angel she needed time to think about it. She could have worried about what others would think, or how this could ruin her reputation. She might have worried about losing Joseph or any other potential suitor. But she did not. In fact, Mary replied boldly in Luke 1:38, "Behold, I am a servant of the Lord; let it be to me according to your word." It is reminiscent of Isaiah saying, "Here I am! Send me" in Isaiah 6:8. God already knew he could trust Mary to carry out this great mission, just as the husband of the Proverbs 31 woman can trust his wife to do good deeds for their family without fear or consequences.

A HEART A HUSBAND CAN TRUST

Marriage is not an easy task. Upon entering that relationship, you are suddenly responsible for the emotional and spiritual well-being of your husband in a unique way. You also allow your own spiritual and emotional needs to be nurtured by him. It is not a covenant to be entered into lightly or a relationship that should be allowed to grow stale. Besides the relationship we have with God, it is the most important one we have. In fact, as we read Proverbs 31, we notice that the relationship the ideal woman has with her husband is essential to every other aspect of her character. It is because of her love for her family that she brings in food from afar and is prepared to face the future. Driven by love for her family, she shows them honor. We too must cultivate this love for our husbands so that his heart will trust in us.

When you have a husband that does not trust in you, your marriage will fall apart. If he cannot trust you to provide good things for your family, he will not trust your ability to handle money. If you do not work hard for the family's needs, he will not trust you with the children.

If he does not trust your heart, he will not expect you to make the right decisions for the family. Making sure our husbands can trust us is a long-term process. Trust does not come at the first stirrings of affection; it does not come by flattering words or romantic actions. Trust comes when we consistently do the right and loving thing even when it is difficult. Trust comes when we make an effort to keep our promises though other things can hinder or distract us. Trust comes when we understand, support, and help our husband accomplish his goals. When our husband knows that we are his true helpmeet, our relationship will flourish.

The word *helper* (cf. Gen. 2:18, 20) in Hebrew means one who gives assistance. Often, modern-day interpretations of this word make helpmeet sound like a maid or servant instead of an equal partner to our husbands. However, if our husbands cannot trust us, we cannot be his equal partner. We become his partner by having God as the center of our lives. If we both share a common love for the Father and have our eyes fixed on him, then our spiritual growth and health will be the first priority of our marriage. The relationship we have with God before we are married will directly affect the goals of our marriage after the ceremony. The relationship we maintain with the Father after we are married will correlate to the relationship we have with our husbands. God and his law must be the center of both of our lives if we want to be true partners with our husbands.

A HEART GOD CAN TRUST

God asked Mary to do a great deed that would affect everyone for the rest of time. No one else will ever be asked to be the mother of the Son of God again. So how much more faithfully can we carry out the commands that God has given us? When we consider Mary's obedience to God's will versus our own, ours pale in comparison. What has God asked us to do? He has asked us to love him with all our heart, soul, mind, and strength. He told us to love his law and obey his commands. He asked us to love our neighbors as ourselves and to take care of widows and orphans. He asked us to proclaim his Name to all the world and to baptize those who believe in him. But we do not always do these things. We are afraid of what others will think if we preach too loudly. We are too selfish to take in those that may need our love and support. Rather than follow God's law, we follow the whims of our hearts wherever they may lead.

So how do we become like Mary? How do we have a relationship with God so that his heart trusts in us?

First, we begin by knowing his Word. God has revealed himself to us in a very powerful and concrete way. The Scriptures have been recorded so that we may not only know his law and what he expects from us, but who he is and the desires of his heart. By reading the Bible, we learn things about God that he has made known. Just as a young wife studies and listens to her husband's needs, desires, and passions, we find those same things written in God's Word. By reading the creation account, we know that God is a God of love, order, and relationship. We see in his dealings with the Israelites that he is a God of justice, forgiveness, and protectiveness. Because of his laws, we know that God values fairness, honesty, and purity. We also know he values our holiness above all else.

If we want to honor God, then the things he cherishes must also be cherished by us. The goals and passions he has for his creation, we must also have for the world. A wife who serves alongside her husband will only accomplish their goals if they are the same and if the husband and wife work together in harmony. In the same way, only when our priorities line up perfectly with the Father's will, will we begin to understand who he is and be able to work effectively in his kingdom.

Second, we must spend time in prayer. If we want to earn the Father's trust, we must be honest in his presence. Prayer allows us to open our hearts and minds to him. In prayer, we can petition the Father to find work that will honor him, to create in us a righteous heart, and to protect us from sin. So often, we come in prayer seeking healing from difficult situations or begging for blessings in our lives. However, when we read the Lord's prayer (what some call the Model Prayer) in Matt. 6:9, the first line says: "Our Father in heaven, hallowed be your name." Rarely do we pray or even consider these words. Most of the time, we ignore what the Father wants, but any good wife and servant of the King knows that our greatest desire should be for his good and not just our own. By seeking his guidance in the work we are supposed to do, we are signaling to him that we are ready to work for him, so that when God calls us, we can say boldly to him as Mary did, "Let it be to me according to your word" (Luke 1:38).

Third, if we want God to trust in us, we have to be obedient in the little things. Throughout the Bible, there are commands given by the Lord on how we should live each day. If we cannot follow these commands, how can we expect God to call us to something greater? If we do not love our husbands in the small, daily things, how can we expect him to love and trust us when it comes to the major things?

The story of the talents is a good example of this. The parable in Matt. 25:14-30 tells of three servants and their master. Each of the servants are given a sum of money to steward while the master is away. The first servant is given five talents, the second servant is given two, and the third servant is given one. The first two servants both double their talents, but the last servant simply buries his, hoping not to lose it. God was not proud of the last servant. In fact, the master in the parable says in vv. 29-30, "For to everyone who has will more be given, and he will have an abundance. But from the one who has not, even what he has will be taken away. And cast the worthless servant into the outer darkness." God expects things from us. He expects us to use what we have and for his glory. When we do not use those things for his glory—whether they be talents, abilities, or possessions—how can we expect him to help us do even bigger and better things?

God trusted Mary because she had been a faithful servant. He honored her by giving her one of the greatest tasks ever commanded. By being faithful to him, we too will be blessed by his presence in our lives. We start by choosing each day to follow him no matter the circumstances. That is probably the hardest part of being faithful. It is easy to be faithful when conditions are easy, or when we are surrounded by others that have chosen to be dedicated to God. It is not so easy when others criticize us or doubt our sincerity. It is difficult to be faithful when the trials of life bear down on us. How can we be faithful to a God that will allow a child to get sick and die? How can we be faithful when those around us abuse us and beat us down? There are many tough questions that can deter us from developing a strong faith, and there are often not many answers. Despite the difficulties this life has to offer, we must choose to be faithful anyway.

By choosing faithfulness, especially in the hard times, we become a treasured woman. Our very actions show that we believe in a God who will take care of us and help us endure all things. By remaining faithful, we will prove that we have a God who is bigger than our problems and is greater than our sin. If Mary had accepted the job God had given her, but later had renounced her faith or spoken badly about her difficulties, would we have considered her act so courageous? Would she have shown how great God was or how petty and selfish humanity truly is? Mary is treasured, not just because she bore the Son of Man, but because she did so admirably and humbly. Our faith through the difficulties of life is just one more way we can show the world how excellent our God really is.

DISCUSSION QUESTIONS:

1. How do you think Mary felt when Gabriel came and spoke to her?

2. How would you have reacted in Mary's place?

3. What holds you back from obeying God's commands?

4. What are some things you can learn about God by reading and meditating on his Word?

5. How can prayer build a relationship with God?

6. What are some talents in your life that you are using for God or could use for God?

7. How can using your talents or simple obedience bring you closer to Him?

3

MARY & MARTHA

LUKE 10:38-42

She considers a field and buys it... — Prov. 31:16

House-hunting can be a fun, though difficult, process. We all want the perfect house—one in which we can see our family growing and thriving. So we do not begin the process lightly. We set a criteria that each house must meet in order to be our dream home. Is it located near my workplace or good schools? Are there enough bedrooms? Does the layout fit my family's needs? Will there be a good resale value? Does it need work? And many, many more questions can plague us during the house-hunting process.

It is not unlike the treasured woman of Proverbs 31. In v. 16, it says, "She considers a field and buys it." When we consider something, we think about it. We mull it over in our heads and try to predict the impact of that decision. The Proverbs 31 woman is noted for her decision-making skills. She goes out to the land and considers a particular field. She may have asked herself questions like, *Will it be profitable for my family to buy this field? Will I plant a new crop? Can that crop be successful here? Can I do the work it will take to harvest the crop?* In the same way, when we make decisions, we must ask ourselves, *Is this a good decision for my family, and can I honor God by the choice I make?*

HONORING GOD

We may not always think that the decisions we make on a daily basis are as significant as buying a house or a field, but honoring God by what we do should be at the very heart of every decision we make. Each day, we choose whether to be at work or home. We choose the people with whom we associate and the activities in which we get involved. Each day, we consider fields and whether they will be profitable for us, our families, and for God.

In the account of Mary and Martha in Luke 10:38-42, we see a similar situation. The field Mary purchases isn't land to plant a vineyard, but simply a spot near the feet of Jesus to sit and listen. Mary could have easily been in the kitchen cleaning or preparing a meal. She could have pleased her sister or impressed the apostles with her homemaking skills, but instead she chose to sit at the feet of Jesus and glean from his knowledge. Like the treasured woman of Proverbs 31, Mary decided which place would be most beneficial for her. She thought about it and took advantage of a promising situation. We see at the end of the passage that her efforts were rewarded when Jesus praises her in v. 42, "One thing is necessary. Mary has chosen the good portion, which will not be taken away from her."

ONE THING NECESSARY

The one thing that is necessary is the Lord's instruction. It is more important than the possessions we have, the jobs we do, or the passions we indulge. Unfortunately, we allow the things of the world to cloud our judgments. Like Martha, we get caught up in the busyness of our days and what we think has to be done, and we do not consider the fields of opportunity and buy them. Jesus offered both Mary and Martha the chance to learn. They both had the space and the time to sit at Jesus' feet and listen just like the Proverbs 31 woman had a chance to buy a field. Both the treasured woman and Mary took advantage of the opportunity and acted on it. Martha not only threw her chance away, but she whined that Mary had not done the same.

We often fall victim to the influences of the world. Mary could have easily listened to Martha and spent time doing the tasks that needed to be done instead of taking time to learn and commune with the Lord. We see a house that needs to be cleaned and skip going to church. We see our kids wanting toys and give our extra portions to their desires instead of the needs of those who are truly hurting. We try to impress those around us and forget that, in the grand scheme of life, only one thing is necessary.

Mary could have seen this time as a chance to impress the disciples. Maybe she was longing for a husband and trying to catch one of their eyes. She could have made delicious food or spent time parading herself around as she cleaned the house. But she chose to focus her attention on the Lord. How many of us make decisions that are not the best financially or ethically, but will go a long way in impressing those around us? How many of us make decisions hoping to get the attention of others and forget to put our focus on God? In all things, the Lord will take care of us, but the rest of the world will not.

In Phil. 4:11-12, the apostle Paul writes, "I have learned in whatever situation I am to be content. I know how to be brought low, and I know how to abound. In any and every circumstance, I have learned the secret of facing plenty and hunger, abundance and need." We often look at those verses to soothe ourselves for not having what we want. We want to be reminded that God loves us and will take care of us whether we are rich or poor.

However, the passage is not necessarily teaching us to be happy with our circumstances, but rather to be so focused on God and his work that our circumstances do not matter. If our main priority is doing the Lord's work, then so much of what we have will not matter. Our food will be used to feed the hungry instead of bloating our bellies. Our houses will be used to serve others instead of castles built for our pleasure. Our choices will be easier to make because they are grounded in God's service. Despite all that goes into making some decisions, if the Lord is our main priority, if his will and commands are our main goals, and if our desires are the same as his, then we will know which fields should be bought and from which to walk away.

IN THE SMALL THINGS

Not every decision will be as momentous as purchasing a field or take as much consideration as buying a house. But the decisions of what we wear, how we spend our time, and the words that come out of our mouth all have the potential to be life-changing. We can never be sure how the smallest gesture will influence someone around us. If we stand around at work gossiping and putting our coworkers down, who around us will know that we follow a greater God? Paul says in Eph. 4:29, "Let no corrupting talk come out of your mouths, but only such as is good for building up, as fits the occasion, that it may give grace to those who hear."

If we show up to our children's school or ball field dressed immodestly, what example will we set for our children? What signals do short shorts give to other fathers? What does our dress suggest about our relationship with our husband? Does our appearance tell the world that the heart of our husband can trust in us? Peter reminds us, "Do not let your adorning be external—the braiding of hair and the putting on of gold jewelry, or the clothing you wear— but let your adorning be the hidden person of the heart with the imperishable beauty of a gentle and quiet spirit, which in God's sight is very precious" (1 Pet. 3:3-4).

Do we spend our time in places that honor God? Do our children think we would rather be out shopping than spending time with them? No matter how small, at the heart of every decision is whether we are using this opportunity for our benefit or for God's glory. If we will intentionally follow the guidelines Jesus left in his Word, and if we are faithful in making decisions that follow his will in the small things, then when we are faced with bigger decisions, they will not be so difficult to make. By choosing the godly things in the small things, we will not as often be faced with the tough decisions of life.

HAVING A SPIRIT OF FORGIVENESS

While our goal is to constantly choose the good things, it is also not to pick the bad things. Too many times, we choose sin over righteousness, anger over concern, hate instead of love. Sometimes, in order to choose the right thing, we have to let go of bad things. We cannot have a prosperous faith if we are harboring feelings of ill-will or bitterness. When someone has hurt us, we must choose forgiveness, no matter how attractive anger or hate may seem. The more we concentrate on the bad things, the less time we have for the good things. If we are nurturing our fields of hate and bitterness, we cannot tend to our gardens of love and wisdom. If we spend time thinking about the hurt that has been done to us, we cannot focus on the blessings God has granted us. If we do not forgive when we approach God, we will be covered in the filth of sin and hatred. Our hearts will be far from the purity God expects from us.

In fact, in Mark 11:25, Jesus instructs his listeners to be forgiving: "And whenever you stand praying, forgive, if you have anything against anyone, so that your Father also who is in heaven may forgive you your trespasses." We must forgive. By choosing not to forgive, God will not forgive our own sins. Just as the treasured woman of Proverbs 31 considered a field and whether it was good or bad, we must forgo the fields of anger and resentment. It's not always easy; it will take a conscious effort on our part to walk away from those feelings and embrace a spirit of forgiveness. However, choosing forgiveness is a choice we will never regret. Choosing forgiveness is also mirroring our Father. When people see us forgive, they will see the love of God shining through us. They will see our character of mercy and know we are citizens of God's kingdom, true imitators of the nature of Christ.

NO REGRETS

Just as Martha was told that Mary had made the right choice, and that it would not be taken away from her, our good choices cannot be taken away from us. If the field the woman bought was productive, then she would never regret buying it. If we choose to do the right thing, then we will never regret making that choice. But like the Proverbs 31 woman, we must consider our fields. She probably considered all the ramifications of the field and her options, and then she made a well-informed decision. We cannot go to a land office and get the specs on our life. However, we can go to the Word. Psalm 119:105 says, "Your word is a lamp to my feet and a light to my path." No matter what decisions face us, no matter what problems or situations land in our lives, the Bible can give us the guidance we need to make a well-informed decision. While the outcomes of our decisions may not always appear profitable, we will nonetheless never regret doing the right thing.

Unfortunately, the right answers we seek to our problems will not come from other people, especially those that do not have a heart that seeks after God. The right answers will not necessarily be the ones touted by the Internet or by knowledgeable people. Only in the Word can we find the answers that will calm our hearts and help us build the right relationship with the Lord.

Many, if not all, of us would give a great deal in exchange to sit at Jesus' feet for a few hours and learn from him. Martha probably did not realize the treasure she had in her home that day. She was too worried about the bread in her oven to realize that in her home sat the Bread of Life. Too often, we can let all the other stuff in life cloud our vision. Many of us also have the bread of life in our homes. It is not the flesh and bones of Jesus's body, but a leather-bound book with the Words of Life. We must take the time to read it. We must choose to put down our brooms and walk away from a dirty sink and open the Word. If we do not take advantage of the Bible, how can we ever expect to listen to Jesus? Our time with the Lord is very special. Martha may not have realized how little time Jesus actually had on earth. Had she known his death and ascension were so near, would she have made a different choice? Would she have even considered the physical food?

Mary and the treasured woman of Proverbs 31 had a goal. They each had something they wanted, they considered their decisions, and they made their goals happen. We can be like Mary and the Proverbs 31 woman. By making sure our priorities line up with the Father's, we too can choose fields that will be profitable for both us and the Father. But we must consider him in all we do.

DISCUSSION QUESTIONS:

1. What are some big "fields" we consider today?

2. What things help you make your decisions?

3. Is it easy for us to use the Bible in our decision-making?

4. What are some things you regret making decisions about?

5. Which verses in the Bible do you go to in order to make some of your decisions easier?

6. In addition to the Bible, the wise counsel of older Christians can help us tremendously in the decision-making process. How have they bought their fields?

4

PRISCILLA, LOIS, & EUNICE

ACTS 18; 2 TIMOTHY 1:5

With the fruit of her hands she plants a vineyard... — Prov. 31:16

Few objects are as powerful as the seed. Each seed has the potential to become the food we eat, wood to shelter us, fabric to clothe us, or color to beautify our lives. We could not survive without seeds. However, there is nothing grand or eye-catching about a seed; a seed's power lies only in its potential. Without knowing what a seed is, we would quickly sweep up that hard, tiny speck into a dustbin and throw it in the trash. But once we realize what a seed can do for us, we take great care to nurture it. We plant that small seed into the ground with careful hands. We feed and water that tiny speck. We are careful to make sure it gets sunlight and shade. We take care of it, hoping that it will grow big, beautiful, and fruitful.

In Prov. 31:16, the treasured woman plants a vineyard with her hands. She takes care of the vineyard from its tiny seeds to the full-grown plants. From that vineyard, she has grapes to make wine, food to eat, and products to sell in the marketplace. She is not afraid to get her hands dirty or sweat through the day in order to see her task come to fruition. She does not give up on the vineyard simply because the work has become difficult. The vineyard is just another example of her desire to provide for her family and to do so well.

PLANTING OUR VINEYARDS

As New Testament Christians, we know we do not just need physical food, but the spiritual food of God's Word. Like our physical food, our spiritual food starts with the seed of knowledge. That seed must also be planted, fed, nurtured, and helped to maturity. And like the physical seed of a giant tree, the spiritual seed's power lies mostly in its potential. The Proverbs 31 woman recognized the potential of a vineyard for her family and community. We must acknowledge that each seed of knowledge we plant in the life of those around us has the power to change that person's world.

Three women in the New Testament took the time to plant seeds of faith: Priscilla, the wife of Aquila, Lois, the grandmother of the missionary Timothy, and Eunice, Timothy's mother. These three women taught the gospel to those in need. They taught when the work was difficult, but they pressed on to see their work through to the end. In turn, their faith has been recorded for us to study and emulate centuries later. We too can evangelize those who need the gospel. It may take time and energy. We may have to get our hands dirty, but there will be nothing more satisfying in the end than knowing we planted a seed of faith in someone's soul, and God will cause the increase.

GETTING DIRTY

As beautiful as the Proverbs 31 woman is described, we know she was not afraid to get her hands dirty and do the hard work that planting a vineyard requires. As women, we must be prepared to do the hard and sometimes dirty work of planting a spiritual vineyard of God's people. We all have special ways to spread the gospel. We can reach out to our friends and neighbors like Priscilla. Or we can evangelize through the special calling we have to raise our children in the Lord like Lois and Eunice. Thankfully, the Bible has given us examples of how they planted their seeds.

In Acts 18, we read Priscilla's story. In v. 2, we learn that Paul the apostle came to stay with her and her husband, Aquila. This part of Priscilla's story is often overlooked. She and her husband welcomed Paul into their home. Not only did they provide him lodging but an opportunity to work with them in their tent-making business. Priscilla was an encouragement to Paul and became his caretaker. They could have allowed Paul to stay somewhere else. They could have used Paul's shady past as an excuse not to trust him or even welcome him into their community. However, Priscilla saw Paul's potential and nurtured it.

Like Priscilla, we must recognize the life-changing effect the gospel can have on every person. No matter where we are in our spiritual walk—whether we are new, struggling Christians or older, mature Christians—we all need encouragement to remain faithful in difficult times. Priscilla did that for Paul. We too can be hospitable to those who are missionaries, preachers, or teachers. Our encouragement and help to them can go a long way in nurturing their souls to be more fruitful in the kingdom. In Gal. 6:10, we see this is commanded for us: "So then, as we have opportunity, let us do good to everyone, and especially to those who are of the household of faith." We do not know what potential our seeds of kindness can do for those around us, especially for ministers of the gospel.

Fortunately, Priscilla's story of faith continues. We read in Acts 18:18 that she, Aquila, and Paul leave for Syria. They were not going on vacation or to see the sights. They left for Syria to specifically spread the gospel. The Great Commission found in Matt. 28:19, "Go therefore and make disciples of all nations, baptizing them in the name of the Father and of the Son and of the Holy Spirit," was meant for all of us. Like the treasured woman, Priscilla sought to plant a vineyard. The vineyard would not harvest grapes or wine, but souls for the Kingdom. It too would take hard work, setbacks, and much nurturing, but the potential would be world-changing. We must also be willing to go and spread the gospel and harvest our own vineyards. Luckily, we live in a time when evangelism has been made easier. There are numerous Bible studies, videos, and other resources that can help us lead a person to Christ. We just have to be willing.

Once Aquila and Priscilla arrived in Ephesus, they went to the synagogue to hear the preacher Apollos. While Apollos knew much about Jesus and his love, he only knew the baptism of John. In Acts 18:26, the Bible says they took Apollos aside and taught him more accurately. In order for Priscilla to teach the Word more accurately, she had to know what the Word said. Once again, our knowledge and understanding of the Scriptures are paramount to our spiritual development. We are not just called to understand, but to put those words into practice. Priscilla helped correct Apollos and, by doing so, enabled Apollos to go out and spread the gospel even further. The potential number of those who came to know the Lord because of Priscilla's faith, knowledge, and willingness to teach could have been quite large. No seed is so small that its effect cannot be felt for years to come.

NURTURING OUR VINEYARDS

For those of us who have children in our lives, the seeds can be much more potent. As we raise and influence our children, we have no idea what they will be able to accomplish for the Kingdom of God. Lois and Eunice are excellent examples of this. Not only did they raise a faithful child; they raised a child who went with Paul and won many souls for Christ. In 2 Tim. 1:5, Paul wrote these words of encouragement, "I am reminded of your sincere faith, a faith that dwelt first in your grandmother Lois and your mother Eunice and now, I am sure, dwells in you as well." Lois and Eunice taught Timothy. The Bible does not say exactly how they taught. They could have schooled him under the tutelage of great scholars or read the Scriptures to him daily. But whatever they did, they showed sincere faith.

Sincere faith requires us to guard our heart and keep it close to the Father. If we want children to know God and his love, then our faith must be real and enduring. We cannot tell our children that they are gifts from above and then not treat them with the love and discipline God intended. We cannot teach our children to love others if we criticize others and make fun of them. We cannot teach our children the glorious nature of God if we do not appreciate it in our own lives. A sincere faith means we do not just put it on for show or to be part of a club. A sincere faith will be the guiding and motivating force of all we do.

In order for us to have a sincere faith, we must draw close to the Lord and make sure our children know we belong to him. Our children need to see us studying the Word of God. They need to see us reach out to those who do not have Christ in their life and help them discover the blessings of Christianity. Our children need to see us desiring to be at worship and kneeling in prayer. Our children need to see us so in love with the Father that we depend on him for every need, rely on his wisdom, and shape our lives around his commands. The greatest way to convince our children of the love of God is not in some program or curriculum; the greatest way to convince our children is to be convinced ourselves. We are the greatest object lesson of living a life pleasing to the Lord.

There is no greater legacy, possession, or name we can give our children than that of Christian. In a society where Sunday school curriculum, books, the Internet, and even copies of the Bible are prevalent, biblical knowledge can easily be acquired. However, biblical knowledge can never replace spiritual maturity. Spiritual maturity can only be acquired when our Bible knowledge combines with our spiritual sincerity. We can have lots of passion for God, but if we do not have the knowledge to shape that passion, our vineyards will not grow. However, we can also have lots of biblical knowledge and no passion to spread the Word of God. It takes both to make a vineyard grow. It takes love and sincerity to save the lost.

The treasured woman of Proverbs 31 planted a vineyard. She grew that vineyard with love, dedication, and hard work. It takes all three to save the world. The Proverbs 31 woman was praised because she planted a physical, fruit-bearing vineyard of grapes. By teaching others about God, we can plant a spiritual, fruit-bearing vineyard of souls. How powerful is that! When others, especially our children, see that dedication in us, they will see that we are different. They will know the priorities we have set are for a greater purpose. And in turn, our lives can be a living testament to the Father's love, grace, and faithfulness.

DISCUSSION QUESTIONS:

1. What would the Proverbs 31 woman or any gardener have to do in order to get a vineyard ready for harvest?

2. How can we take those same skills she used in planting a vineyard and translate them into saving souls?

3. How can we use the Parable of the Sower in Luke 8:1-15 to prepare ourselves to plant seeds of knowledge?

4. Which aspect of Priscilla's story would you find easy to incorporate into your spiritual life?

5. Which would you find difficult?

6. How can you overcome those difficulties?

7. In your home and community, how can you best pass on your faith to those around you?

5

TABITHA

ACTS 9:36-43

She opens her hand to the poor and reaches out her hands to the needy. – Prov. 31:20

Reaching out to others is scary. We never know how other people will react to our intentions. We may fear that they will reject our help or take advantage of us. We may find they are not appreciative of our actions. We may discover that our actions do not really help them at all. Add to that list busy schedules, needy children, and other priorities, and women can easily find excuses to stay inside their bubbles and not reach out to the less fortunate.

But the treasured woman of Proverbs 31 does not make excuses. Rather, she makes it a priority to reach out to others. In spite of all her familial obligations, she still takes time to think about those who are poor and needy. She recognizes their needs and supplies them, and we must cultivate this quality in our lives as well. All around us, people are suffering. They may lack physical needs such as food and clothing, or they may lack the spiritual blessings of love and encouragement. It is our job to learn to recognize these needs and find ways of fulfilling them.

STITCHING TOGETHER LOVE AND HONOR

One such woman who exemplified this quality of reaching out to the poor is the disciple Tabitha. The meaning of the word *disciple* in this passage has been heavily debated for a long time. We do know that her life embodied the teachings of Jesus and the very nature of his compassion for others. Tabitha had found a way to fill both spiritual and physical needs with one of the special gifts God had blessed her with. Tabitha was a seamstress; she made beautiful garments for those who did not have any. By giving away these garments, she also gave those who received them honor and respect. She showed them the love of Christ through her gifts, which softened their hearts and pointed them to the Father. We can easily see how many of those widows would become followers of Christ simply because she took the time to sew something for them.

The widows' appreciation and devotion to Tabitha is so strong that when she died in Acts 9:36, those who mourned her rushed to the apostle Peter and pled with him to raise her from the dead. When Peter came to visit Tabitha's body, the mourners showed him the fruit of her hands. They were so proud of the garments she had made for them and the honor she had shown them that they could not stop showing off her creations. So often, when we give to the poor, we give our leftovers. We give our children's outgrown clothes or the things we are going to discard anyway. Tabitha took the time to make things for the poor that were beautiful and specifically for them. She took time to honor them with the Spirit of Christ.

When looking at Tabitha more in-depth, we will discover a few things. First, it was thought that she was a widow and possible wealthy. Her husband is not mentioned among the mourners, just other widows, and she evidently had the means to make clothes for those who could not provide for themselves. With this knowledge, we may look at our own situations and think we cannot possibly do what Tabitha did.

Many of us have children, husbands, or others who depend on us and demand our time. Our finances are tied up in our own families and homes. We can't just stop all that we do or give all that we have to others. But can we a give a part, and can we do it with grace?

Unlike Tabitha, the Proverbs 31 woman had a family and responsibilities. She was planting vineyards and buying food from afar. She was making clothes and building her arms with strength. But when she had a chance, she reached out to the poor. She made it part of her routine and included it in her family provisions. She also did it in a way that respected the poor. Both Tabitha and the treasured woman of Proverbs 31 loved people enough to make room in their budgets, schedules, and hearts for those who needed a little bit more or could not provide for themselves. Neither woman made excuses for their responsibility to the poor. They were not turned away from the grotesque nature of the poor. They did not look down with haughty eyes at those who could not provide for themselves. Instead, they rose to meet the challenge and honored with grace and love those who had little.

We cannot all be dressmakers like Tabitha, but we all have talents we can use to help others. Fortunately, being part of a church family may offer us more opportunities to help those who are less fortunate. Instead of just giving our leftovers to the church's clothes closet, we can buy or make new things. We can help those who are sick by offering our time and resources. We can find organizations within our community (e.g. Meals on Wheels, school supply drive) that help others and make it part of our family's mission. We cannot all be like Tabitha and devote our entire lives to the poor as she did. We do, however, need to be aware of the needs around us, and not only find ways to meet those needs, but make it a part of our life to continuously help those who are suffering.

LEARNING TO LOVE THE UNLOVABLE

However, whether we can give of our means or time is secondary to learning to love those who are in need or hurting. We will never truly help people if we never learn to love them. Jesus said in Matt. 25:44-45, "Then they also will answer, saying, 'Lord, when did we see you hungry or thirsty or a stranger or naked or sick or in prison, and did not minister to you?' Then he will answer them, saying, 'Truly, I say to you, as you did not do it to one of the least of these, you did not do it to me.'" Each person is part of God's creation and therefore part of the Father. The dirty, downtrodden, grotesque, and sinful are all his children and should be treated as such.

The lesson of Tabitha is not necessarily her resurrection or the beauty of her garments. Her lesson is that she learned to love those who were unlovable. Part of planting seeds into the lives of other people is knowing the state of their hearts. If they are hurting financially, physically, or spiritually, then at the very least, our hearts can hurt with them and share the love of God with them. Sharing God's love may mean providing for their needs physically, but it certainly means telling them about God, how much he cares for them, and how he can save them spiritually.

Earlier in Matt. 25:35-40, Jesus said, "For I was hungry and you gave me food, I was thirsty and you gave me drink, I was a stranger and you welcomed me, I was naked and you clothed me, I was sick and you visited me, I was in prison and you came to me.' Then the righteous will answer him, saying, 'Lord, when did we see you hungry and feed you, or thirsty and give you drink? And when did we see you a stranger and welcome you, or naked and clothe you? And when did we see you sick or in prison and visit you?' And the King will answer them, 'Truly, I say to you, as you did it to one of the least of these my brothers, you did it to me.'"

Think of the people who came to know God just through Tabitha's death. Think of how many people came to understand God's love through her good works, especially those who needed it the most. For thousands of years, people have read the account of Tabitha's death and have been inspired by the miracle of her resurrection. But more importantly, they have been encouraged to become women that crowds beg to have resurrected after death.

Tabitha, through her good works, proved herself to be a treasured woman. By loving the people she came in contact with, even those that were poor and dirty, she gave value to each person just as God has given value to everyone simply by their existence. She also forgave the sinful. Could we make a beautiful garment of clothing for a liar or a gossiper or a scoundrel? If we truly want to honor God with our lives, we must honor his creation. Each of us is special and unique because we are made by him, and each one of us depends on his glory and his grace. To shun a person because they are not like us, to hide the love of the Father because we think they are not worthy, to assume that we are better than they, or feel that our lives are more valuable than theirs is a sad representation of what God has done for us. God made each one of us equal. In turn, our lives—no matter how small, poor, or disabled—can show the love of God through our actions and behavior towards those around us.

STANDING BEFORE THE LORD

We all need God. We all depend on his righteousness and justice. On the Day of Judgment, we will all stand before the Father as equals. None of us will sit at the front as prized citizens of heaven. None of us will have bought our way there, and none of us will have earned a spot in heaven. The Father will judge all of us by whether we gave our lives to him. Part of giving our lives to him is showing love to everyone he created. By giving to the least of these, we give to the Father. No matter what season of life we are in, poor students just starting out in life, young wives and mothers, experienced business women, or that wonderful, older sister, we can still take time to love those around us and provide for them the best we can.

Reaching out to the poor can be scary. People will not react the way we hope. Some will reject us, take advantage of us, or never say thank you. However, in their time of need and desperation, we can be a ray of love, friendship, and giving in their dark world. No matter what their response is to us, our response to them should be loving and point the way to the Father. By pointing back to the Father, we show how much love and grace the Father has to offer. We have no idea what our actions might mean to the suffering. Tabitha taught people the love of Christ through her actions. She honored the Father by giving to those who needed something she had to offer.

Let us do the same.

DISCUSSION QUESTIONS:

1. What are some ways you can help the poor or the unfortunate in your town, community, or church?

2. In your season of life, how can you help the less fortunate?

3. What is your reaction to the poor?

4. Does that help or hinder you from helping when you can?

5. What holds you back from making charity work part of your life?

6. How can you help the poor in a spiritual way?

6

RUTH, NAOMI'S DAUGHTER-IN-LAW

RUTH 1:1-22

She dresses herself with strength and makes her arms strong...
– Prov. 31:17

In the opening verses of the book of Ruth, we discover that it took place in the time of the Judges, an especially difficult period for the Lord's people. They were caught in a constant cycle of rebellion, punishment, and deliverance. Poverty, illness, and death were prevalent throughout the land. For Ruth, these things were especially close since she and Naomi, her precious mother-in-law, were destined to lead lives of destitution. Her husband, father-in-law, and brother-in-law had all died, leaving the women with no male leadership or protection. There were no jobs for women, meaning there was no way she could make it on her own. Even Naomi had given up. She wanted to change her name to *Mara* (meaning bitter), go back to the land of Israel, and die. Things did not look promising for Ruth.

When Naomi announced she was going back home, she pleaded with Ruth to return to her parent's house. At least there, she would be in her father's care and might find a new husband. But Ruth said, "No."

She loved Naomi. She would remain faithful to her. Some of the most loving words of the Bible are recorded in Ruth 1. When she pledges her life to Naomi, she says in v. 16, "Do not urge me to leave you or to return from following you. For where you go I will go, and where you lodge I will lodge. Your people shall be my people, and your God my God."

KEEPING A COVENANT

It is hard to read the verses in Ruth 1 and not feel the conviction Ruth had to follow Naomi. But keeping those promises would be hard. Ruth and Naomi were going to a place where they had no male guardian, which in those days was essential for a woman's survival. There was no one to financially take care of them. If Ruth and Naomi were to survive, then Ruth would have to work very hard. She would have to find them lodging. She would have to gather in other people's fields after the gleaners and harvesters had already been through. She would get only the leftovers. Ruth may have to marry just to keep Naomi and herself alive. Ruth knew this, however. She knew going back to Naomi's home would be challenging and difficult, but she went anyway. She went because she loved Naomi, and she trusted that God would take care of them.

Ruth also knew the value of hard work. She would work long hours just to keep herself and Naomi fed. The Proverbs 31 woman was also not afraid of hard work. In v. 17, the author writes, "She dresses herself with strength and makes her arms strong." Taking care of our family is hard work, whether it is an elderly parent, a brood of children, or a husband who has many responsibilities. However, whatever our family structure, we have made a commitment to take care of them and honor them. Like Ruth and the treasured woman of Proverbs 31, we should be willing to do whatever it takes to make sure our families are well taken care of.

A LITTLE HARD WORK

The idea of hard work is praised throughout Scripture. In fact, the Bible says that our work is part of our blessing. In Col. 3:23-24, Paul wrote, "Whatever you do, work heartily, as for the Lord and not for men, knowing that from the Lord you will receive the inheritance as your reward. You are serving the Lord Christ." God gave each of us talents and abilities that he expects us to use. By working hard for him and our families, we will reap the benefits. However, Paul takes hard work a little further for women. In 1 Tim. 2:9, he exhorts young Timothy to teach women that it is not their outward appearance that should gain them attention but their good works. But how many of us fuss and worry about what we or our children wear each Sunday? We may go through a half-dozen outfits and fail to think about the state of our heart before worship.

Our works should make us known to our community and the ones we love. James wrote, "But someone will say, 'You have faith and I have works.' Show me your faith apart from your works, and I will show you my faith by my works" (Jas. 2:18). While we are never saved by what we do, those who are faithful to family and the Lord will do good things for them. We often say to those we care about, "Don't just tell me you love me; show me." The same thing applies to our relationship with the Lord. What good are empty words to our husbands, children, parents, friends, and most importantly God, if we never work for their good? Ruth and the Proverbs 31 woman loved their families so much that they became known for their works.

If we want God to know that we love him, we must prove it by our actions. While all of us may do different jobs here on earth, we should all do them for God's glory. By working for him, we show the world that there is something worth living for other than ourselves. Paul wrote so eloquently in Phil. 1:21-22, "For to me to live is Christ, and to die is gain. If I am to live in the flesh, that means fruitful labor for me." That fruitful labor, whatever it may be, is great and wonderful because of the outcome it will have in the Kingdom of God! What are we doing for Christ today?

PRIORITIZING

In biblical times, taking care of the family was a much more strenuous job. Cooking a meal could take several hours instead of just one or two. Women had to go and gather their food, while we run to the grocery store or open our refrigerators. Clothes had to be handmade, not store bought. Laundry was done in a river, not in a washing machine inside the home. The work to get simple household chores done in biblical times was much more involved than any chore we have today.

However, they may have had three items of clothing at their disposal, while many of us have thirty or forty. They had two pots; many of us have twenty. Their homes could often fit nicely inside one of ours. We have traded in our simplicity. Thus, the work we have may not be as grueling, but it is two or three times as much. Plus, we have school schedules and baseball practices, hair appointments and PTA meetings. Our schedules are full; our houses are full; our hands are full. We must ask ourselves, are they full of God? Do we do these things for the good of our family? We cannot trade in being over-worked for hard work. Our children can participate in almost any activity they want. We can join any club, society, or committee of our choosing. But we must ask ourselves, are we working for the Lord? Are we showing the Father our faithfulness by the work we do?

Being involved in something we enjoy is not bad. When we let that something take away from our families and the Lord, however, we are not working for him. Our goal in life is to be like the Father and work for him. In Titus 3, Paul begins the chapter writing these words, "Remind them to be submissive to rulers and authorities, to be obedient, to be ready for every good work, to speak evil of no one, to avoid quarreling, to be gentle, and to show perfect courtesy toward all people. For we ourselves were once foolish, disobedient, led astray, slaves to various passions and pleasures, passing our days in malice and envy, hated by others and hating one another. But when the goodness and loving kindness of God our Savior appeared, he saved us, not because of works done by us in righteousness, but according to his own mercy, by the washing of regeneration and renewal of the Holy Spirit."

Our works do not save us, but it is by our works that we show the Father our love. Letting all the other things in life distract us from serving God tells him that he is not as important to us as our mouths would suggest.

WORK IS OUR BLESSING

God has given us many blessings. Have we ever considered that our work is also a blessing for us? The menial tasks we have as women never seem to end. There is rarely a day when we do not have laundry, dishes, or errands. Our children need feeding, and our floors need sweeping. We need to make money and educate our children. There is work to be done for our church family and for the needy. It is true that a woman's work is never done. Paul reminds us in Phil. 2:14-15, "Do all things without grumbling or disputing, that you may be blameless and innocent, children of God without blemish in the midst of a crooked and twisted generation, among whom you shine as lights in the world." Like Ruth, our hard work does not go unnoticed. Our children will watch us. Others in our community and church families will see what we do. If we are going about our work with joy, then others will see that the work we do is done with love for them and for God.

There is no denying Ruth loved Naomi, and she worked hard to ensure her health and well-being. The treasured woman of Proverbs 31 builds herself up so that she can work hard for her family. All of us are called to work hard, whether we are single women serving only the Lord, a mother working to protect her children, or a wife helping her husband. The description of the Proverbs 31 woman building herself up with strength is something we can all do. The harder we work for the Lord and the good of his creation, the more blessings we will receive. John 12:26 says, "If anyone serves me, he must follow me; and where I am, there will my servant be also. If anyone serves me, the Father will honor him." But more important than our own honor is the honor we will bring to the Father by working hard for him. God gave us the ability to work. Let's use it.

DISCUSSION QUESTIONS:

1. How are you working for the Lord?

2. How can you work more diligently?

3. What things distract us from serving the Lord?

4. How can we overcome those distractions?

5. What benefits are there from hard work? Spiritually? Physically? Mentally? Emotionally?

6. Do we have the same loyalty to the people in our lives and to God as Ruth had for Naomi?

7. What do you think prompted that loyalty?

8. How can we cultivate a sense of loyalty like that for God?

7

RUTH, BOAZ'S WIFE

RUTH 2-4

Her husband is known in the gates when he sits among the elders of the land. – Prov. 31:23

Ruth was an extraordinary woman. In fact, she is the only woman described in Scripture with the same word also used to describe the treasured woman of Proverbs 31. In Ruth 3:11, Boaz calls Ruth "worthy." This is the same Hebrew word used in Prov. 31:10: "An excellent wife who can find?" The word "excellent" is the same word Boaz used when he called Ruth "worthy." It means a woman of valor and is often used to describe a woman who is in battle or has shown a lot of courage.

Looking at the life of Ruth, we can see why she was given this description. She trusted the Lord to take care of her and Naomi as they left the land of Moab and returned to Israel. Naomi trusted Ruth and depended on her for her care. She was a woman who made good and righteous decisions, and she then stuck to those decisions. She had not been talked out of them by Naomi or afraid of what the future might hold. Because of her faith and heart, Ruth did virtuous things.

Like Ruth, the Proverbs 31 woman had faith and heart. Unfortunately, the reader is often blind to this treasured woman's value. Her essence is not just in what she accomplishes, but also in her heart that has been given to God, in a love for those around her, and in a faith that will not waiver. Ruth suffered many things. She lost her husband and the other men in her family who might have provided for her. She lost her home. She lost all that was familiar to her. But she faithfully followed Naomi and Naomi's God to a different land. Are we willing to follow our God that far?

FALLING IN LOVE WITH RUTH

The story of Ruth begins ugly and desolate, but ends in one of the most beautiful love stories of the Bible. Once Ruth and Naomi had settled back in Naomi's hometown of Bethlehem, Ruth caught the eye of Boaz. Boaz was a wealthy, knowledgeable man and a distant relative of Naomi. He was well respected in the town, and he sat at the gates among the elders (cf. Prov. 31:23).

What was it about Ruth that made her so attractive to Boaz? When Ruth asked Boaz this very question in 2:10, Boaz replied in vv. 11-12, "All that you have done for your mother-in-law since the death of your husband has been fully told to me, and how you left your father and mother and your native land and came to a people that you did not know before. The LORD repay you for what you have done, and a full reward be given you by the LORD, the God of Israel, under whose wings you have come to take refuge!" Boaz knew her because of her good works, just as the Lord will know us by our works. Boaz also said the Lord would bless Ruth because of her faith and good deeds, just as the Lord will bless us for our faith and good deeds.

We later read about Ruth's desire for Boaz to redeem her, an ancient custom in which a relative would marry a widow so that she could bear children in the name of the family. When Ruth did this, Boaz was quite pleased. He called this kindness greater than the first and gave her the ultimate compliment, saying she was a worthy woman. He accepted her offer and redeemed her. Together, they had a son named Obed, who fathered Jesse, who fathered David, the king of Israel. Thus continued the lineage to Christ. God richly blessed Ruth for her faith and loyalty.

THE BLESSINGS OF FOLLOWING GOD

Being blessed by God does not necessarily mean marriage and childbearing for every woman. Nor does every woman desire it. But God blesses each of us with the promise of a home in heaven. We have a chance to be, not just with a man that sits at the gates, but with the One who created the gates. We have an opportunity to be with the Father for eternity. And while we cannot earn our place there, our good works show the Father just how much we care. In turn, the Lord will bless us. In Luke 12:42-44, Jesus tells his disciples a parable, "Who then is the faithful and wise manager, whom his master will set over his household, to give them their portion of food at the proper time? Blessed is that servant whom his master will find so doing when he comes. Truly, I say to you, he will set him over all his possessions." The more the Lord sees us doing his work, the more he can trust us to do more work and have greater blessings.

Serving God every day is a choice. So often, people need to feel they are called or have a passion for the work of the Lord. In reality, serving God is a choice we make every hour. We decide to serve God in how we choose to spend our time. We choose to serve God in the way we talk to our family and friends. We choose to serve God by the way we approach others, especially those who are in need of love and respect. We choose to serve God by the activities we engage in and the jobs we perform. We choose to serve God when we bow before him in worship and give him glory.

When Boaz tells Ruth that the kindness she is showing him is far greater than the first, the second kindness that Boaz is referring to is her choice in marrying him. Ruth was still young. She could have asked many different men to redeem her, but she chose Boaz. By doing so, she was communicating to Boaz that the loyalty and love she had shown to Naomi, her first kindness, she would now show to him also. She was showing great honor to Boaz. And Boaz, for all of his success and wisdom, recognized this honor and was happy and blessed to redeem Ruth as his wife.

FALLING IN LOVE WITH GOD

When we come to the Lord, offering to redeem our old lives in exchange for one in his service, will he be honored to have us? Do we show love, loyalty, and faithfulness to those in our lives in a way that honors them? Before baptism, we come to the Father sinful and lacking. After baptism, we are forgiven of our sins, cleansed from our old life, and free to live a new life. We understand that, as new Christians, we have a responsibility to live for Christ. Part of committing ourselves to him is living daily for him. Hopefully, we are so in love with Jesus, so committed to his cause, so passionate about his creation that living a life for him is not difficult, or even an after-thought, but an all-consuming passion in our lives.

Falling in love with the Lord may also seem like a daunting task. How can we possibly honor the Great I Am? We fall in love with him the same as we fall in love with people here on earth—we get to know him!

First, we need to study his Word. Being in the Word of God reveals to us his character. Learning the ways of the Lord shows us his immense goodness and justice. Understanding our own weaknesses and failures teaches us the great mercy that he indeed showers upon us. King David wrote in Psa. 1:1-2, "Blessed is the man who walks not in the counsel of the wicked, nor stands in the way of sinners, nor sits in the seat of scoffers; but his delight is in the law of the LORD, and on his law he meditates day and night."

Second, we need to be in constant prayer. Through prayer, we communicate with God. He hears our pleas, and he responds according to our best interest. In Phil. 4:6-7, Paul says, "Do not be anxious about anything, but in everything by prayer and supplication with thanksgiving let your requests be made known to God. And the peace of God, which surpasses all understanding, will guard your hearts and your minds in Christ Jesus." By going to the Father in prayer, we know we can open our hearts to Him. He will hear our pleas and heartaches. He will cover our sins with His blood.

Third, we need to be aware of the blessings he has given us. In Matt. 7:9-11, Jesus reminds us of God's constant love for us: "Or which one of you, if his son asks him for bread, will give him a stone? Or if he asks for a fish, will give him a serpent? If you then, who are evil, know how to give good gifts to your children, how much more will your Father who is in heaven give good things to those who ask him!" By knowing what God has given us, we know God loves us so very much. He gave his Son for us. Recognizing the vastness of his love for us, we cannot help but fall deeper in love with him and his righteousness.

The more we love him, the more we will strive to carry out his will for our lives, to love him with all of our heart, soul, mind, and strength, and to love our neighbor as our self. Doing good things for those we love is easy. Giving good gifts to those we love is not hard. Being committed to their welfare becomes part of our lives. Our lives should mirror that same love for Christ. Boaz was honored by Ruth's desire to be committed to him. The husband of the Proverbs 31 woman was honored by the life his wife led. The Lord will also be honored by our desire to live a life for him. By copying the practices of the Proverbs 31 woman and adopting them in our life, we can become a treasured woman.

When Ruth snuck onto the threshing floor and lay at Boaz's feet, she did so at her own risk. Boaz could have easily taken advantage of her. He could have laughed at her request or ruined her reputation in town. But he did not do so. She came to him humbly and submissively, seeking safety through marriage with him. Because of the worthy life she had chosen to live, Boaz honored her request with great love and tenderness.

When we come humbly to the Father, he also will honor our request. He will provide us with love, peace, and a place among his chosen people in heaven. Like Boaz, the Father in heaven will redeem us as his own. Just as Ruth honored Boaz with her hard work and loyalty, we too can bring glory to God with our hard work and loyalty. All we have to do is choose him.

DISCUSSION QUESTIONS:

1. Boaz was impressed with Ruth's loyalty to Naomi. How did she show this loyalty?

2. Are we called to do the same for the Lord?

3. What made Boaz notice Ruth?

4. How would this influence Boaz?

5. Is it easy to love God?

6. Is it easy to commit our lives to him completely?

7. How can we show God we love him in our lives? In our churches?

8. How important is following God's commands?

8

ABIGAIL

1 SAMUEL 25

Strength and dignity are her clothing… — Prov. 31:25

Life is not always fair. It is filled with hardships and challenges we never thought possible. It is filled with sadness and death that we may feel we cannot handle. Life is filled with obstacles that may seem impossible to overcome. People will disappoint us, take advantage of us, or leave us. Many times, we may simply want to give up. It would be easy to fall into a worldly trap of addictions or anger. We could soothe away our pain or lash out at those who have hurt us, but God has called us to a higher standard.

The Proverbs 31 woman is said to be clothed with strength and dignity. But how can we be clothed with strength and dignity when things around us are not what we want? How can we continue to do good when it seems God has abandoned us to the ugliness of the world? Even more so, how can we continue to do good with strength and dignity? When we continue to do right, even in difficult circumstances, not only will we bless those around us, but we proclaim how excellent our Creator is and how he cares for his people.

DOING GOOD

No one understood the hardships of family life better than Abigail. Abigail was married to a man named Nabal. He was not a dream catch by any stretch of the imagination. Even though he was rich and well known, he was crude and a drunkard. In fact, his very name meant *folly*. He had little respect for other people and certainly none for the Lord and his precepts. When David, the future king of Israel, came to Nabal in need after showing great care for Nabal's men, Nabal rejected David. Of course, David was offended and vowed to take his revenge on Nabal.

When Abigail learned of David's request, Nabal's dismissal, and David's fury, she sprang into action. Immediately, she collected enough food for David's approaching army. She took gifts for him, but more importantly she carried with her a respectful and contrite attitude. When Abigail met David on the road, she dismounted her donkey, walked to David, and fell to her face. The respect and admiration she showed David impressed him so much that he recalled his men and found a place in his heart for this beautiful woman. Abigail was a very wealthy woman, and despite her husband's coarse behavior, was married to a very powerful man. Abigail had no reason to bow before David. At this time, David was an outlaw soldier on the run from Saul. Except for the Lord's blessing, David was in a very precarious circumstance. Abigail did not have to show any respect for David, but she knew the Lord was with him. Upon returning home, Abigail found a very drunk Nabal. She decided to wait until after he had sobered to tell Nabal what she had done. According to 1 Sam. 25:37, when Abigail did tell him, Nabal's heart left him, and he died ten days later.

Throughout the entire ordeal, Abigail acted with a strong sense of goodness, grace, and in a dignified manner. She sought to give David the respect he deserved. While she did not excuse her husband's horrible behavior, she dealt with him in a way that was wise and respectful. Abigail possessed a good sense of right from wrong and treated those with whom she came in contact with a good attitude.

THE MEANING OF DIGNITY

Dignity is a quality we don't always regard with a great deal of esteem. When we are angry, we tend to let everyone know it. When we are mad, we find a great deal of pleasure in debasing those who have offended us. When we think someone is out to get us, we try to become the first to take them out, to beat them to the punch. We act hastily and don't consider the reasons for their actions, much less the consequences of our own. In order to learn how to be dignified, we must look at Abigail, all that she endured, and how she delicately and wisely handled the predicament in which she found herself.

First, Abigail knew the wrong that had been done by her husband and sought to correct it. When Abigail learned that Nabal had rejected David's request, she immediately gathered food and went to him. In 1 Sam 25:18, she "made haste." She did not wait a few days and hope David would forget. Nor did she wait until David's army arrived at her house seeking to kill her husband and his men. Abigail understood that a sin had been committed, and she wanted to make it right. It did not matter that David was an outlaw, that her husband did not respect him, or that he had an army raging behind him. What mattered was a person had been treated poorly by a member of her household, and she took the responsibility to correct it. She welcomed David and his men.

We have all made mistakes. We say things to people that we shouldn't or act in ways that are inappropriate. Proverbs 28:13 says, "Whoever conceals his transgressions will not prosper, but he who confesses and forsakes them will obtain mercy." Do we make haste to correct our wrongs?

Second, when Abigail saw David, she took the blame for her husband's mistakes and demonstrated contrition. She does not excuse her husband from his bad manners; in fact, she tells the truth about him. He is full of folly. However, she took responsibility that David's men were not given better treatment. Abigail could have sought refuge with David and his men and let Nabal and her household parish. Instead, she sought to protect Nabal while being honest about his disposition. She begged forgiveness for her household and gave David the honor he deserved.

We all have the opportunity to say, "I am sorry." But our pride and arrogance often get in the way. We do not want to look weak or appear vulnerable. So many relationships have suffered because we do not take the time to say "I am sorry" anymore. Abigail sought to apologize. In order to be dignified, we have to risk appearing weak. It was Abigail's submissive nature to David and her willingness to make things right that made her attractive to David.

Third, Abigail used discretion. We often look at Nabal and the wrong he did towards David and forget that David was also quick to draw his sword. However, instead of angering David further, Abigail tried to make amends. In 1 Sam. 25:33, David told Abigail, "Blessed be your discretion, and blessed be you, who have kept me this day from bloodguilt and from working salvation with my own hand!" Abigail could have gone to others. She could have told others how awful David was to attack her household. She could have gotten Nabal's men together and attacked David on the road. She could have used angry words and disrespected David and his men even further. Instead, she used her head. She immediately went and apologized and stopped the feud from growing.

Our world craves drama. When given the opportunity, people often use the actions of others to stir up more trouble. Abigail did not. She took the chance of stopping David from doing something horrible. When we have the opportunity to be peacemakers, we should make every effort to do so. Romans 12:18 commands, "If possible, so far as it depends on you, live peaceably with all." Gossiping and talking to others about private matters does not help calm people down. Rather, it stirs more emotions and escalates the tension. By going straight to the source of the tension, Abigail saved the lives of her household, her family's reputation, and showed the grace of our Lord.

Fourth, Abigail was patient. When Abigail returned home, she saw that Nabal was drunk. She did not take the opportunity to berate him or tell of her triumph with David. She waited until her husband was ready to hear her words. Being patient often takes a measure of strength. James tells us, "Know this, my beloved brothers: let every person be quick to hear, slow to speak, slow to anger" (Jas. 1:19). We want people to know when we are right. However, Abigail waited. She wanted Nabal to truly understand her words. By waiting, Nabal was pierced to the heart.

Fifth, Abigail remained centered on the Lord. When Abigail confronted David, she did not say he should not attack Nabal and his men because it would hurt her. She did not whine that she or Nabal did not deserve his retaliation. She did not call David names or rehash his faults. She gently reminded him that he was God's appointed man, and he did not want the guilt of shed blood on his hands. Her focus remained on pleasing God, and her concern was David's righteousness in the sight of the Lord. Once again, we see Abigail rise above her circumstances instead of being mired in distrust and name-calling. By directing David's attention to the Lord, Abigail took his attention away from the trivial matters caused by Nabal. Scholars can make a case that what Nabal had done to David and his men was insolent and culturally unacceptable. David had every right to be angry and offended by Nabal. But it was not David's job to seek revenge. Vengeance belongs to the Lord, both then and now. In order to be strong women like Abigail, our focus must remain on Him. Allowing petty arguments and selfish desires to dictate our attitude does not let the God of the Bible be seen in us. The Lord will deal accordingly with wrong doers. Colossians 3:25 says, "For the wrongdoer will be paid back for the wrong he has done, and there is no partiality." It is not our job to punish those whom we think have wronged us. God has already promised us that he will deal with them. Our job is to remain centered on the Father and, by doing so, point others to him as well.

THE BLESSINGS OF DIGNITY

Because of Abigail's dignity and strength, the Lord blessed Abigail. Because of her appreciation and devotion to the Lord, he gave her a husband also devoted to the Lord, David. Later in 2 Sam. 3:3, we read that Abigail was blessed with a son by David. Abigail's example should inspire our conduct to be better towards those who hurt, persecute, or simply disappoint us. While we should not hope that God will kill off those who mistreat us, we should remember that God will bless us for our actions. Also, we can hope that our actions will bring peace to our families and restore our reputation for good works. We can hope that, by our example, others will follow. On the Day of Judgment, all things shall be revealed, including the good we have done. We will never regret doing the right thing.

We cannot control the actions of others. We cannot always sway their emotions. We cannot bridle their tongues. But we can control ourselves. We should always act in the best way we can. Peter says, "Therefore, beloved, since you are waiting for these, be diligent to be found by him without spot or blemish, and at peace" (2 Pet. 3:14). When others mistreat or threaten us, we should make sure that we have done no wrong. If we have, we should take responsibility for our mistakes and apologize for them. We should not go to others and idly talk about the wrongs they have done, but deal with them directly and with kindness. We should be patient with those who have wronged us. We should allow them time to understand our position and reconcile their wrongs. By imitating Abigail and all that she did, we can be treasured women, full of peace, dignity, and strength.

DISCUSSION QUESTIONS:

1. How do we define dignity?

2. Based on the conversation with David in 1 Sam. 25, what made Abigail strong?

3. What things prevent us from developing strength and dignity?

4. Do we see similarities between our circumstances and Abigail's?

5. What about Abigail's actions do you most admire and hope to mimic in your own life?

6. In a social-media-crazed society, how can we learn to be discreet?

7. What made Abigail attractive to David so that he would want her as his wife?

8. What verses in the Bible can help us be more dignified?

9

DEBORAH

JUDGES 4-5

She opens her mouth with wisdom... — Prov. 31:26

Out of all the character traits we can develop, wisdom is one of the most desired. In fact, Proverbs claims, "Blessed is the one who finds wisdom, and the one who gets understanding, for the gain from her is better than gain from silver and her profit better than gold. She is more precious than jewels, and nothing you desire can compare with her. Long life is in her right hand; in her left hand are riches and honor. Her ways are ways of pleasantness, and all her paths are peace" (Prov. 3:13-17).

As mothers, we always wish to have the perfect words to pass on to our children, words that will have the most impact on their lives. As wives, we wish to know how best to encourage and help our husbands. As Christians, we wish we always had the answers to life's problems. We wish we could do exactly what and how the Lord wants us to do in order to please him. But life is not always black and white. Our children may need to hear things we don't understand. The encouragement our husbands need may be difficult to discern at times. The many decisions we have to face in life are not easy. Our desire to do the right thing may be tested by wanting to do the easy thing. So we pray for wisdom. We pray to do the right thing and hope our decisions have the right outcome.

BECOMING WISE

The treasured woman of Proverbs 31 is described as having wisdom on her lips. The things she said had a great influence on those around her. Another woman in the Bible who was also praised for her wisdom is Deborah. Not much is known about her. We know she is the only female judge to rule in Israel, and she judged for twenty years. We know that she was married to Lapidoth. It is not known if she had children or who her parents were. We do know, however, that she was well respected for her wisdom. People from many miles came to sit at her feet at the Palm of Deborah to hear her judgments and prophecies from the Lord. Her wisdom, however, did not come from her own musings, but by the blessing of God. As a judge, Deborah had been raised up to lead her people. The Bible says in Judg. 2:16, "Then the LORD raised up judges, who saved them out of the hand of those who plundered them." Deborah was wise because she allowed herself to be pliable to the voice of God.

The most well-known judgment she passed was to Barak in his upcoming battle with the Canaanites, their King Jabin, and Canaan's military leader, Sisera. Deborah gave Barak military advice on how to fight the battle, but most importantly warned him that the glory would not be his if he insisted that Deborah accompany him, and that Sisera would be delivered into the hands of a woman, Jael. As the story progresses, we see that Barak is not the hero of the battle, but Jael. Through her quick thinking, she captures Sisera and kills him with a tent peg, thus ending the war with the Canaanites. The important thing to remember is that Deborah was insistent that Barak put his trust in the Lord and not in Deborah. However, Barak wanted her presence. Deborah knew it was not her power or wisdom that would bring victory to the Israelites. And Barak did not receive credit for winning the battle because he had put his faith in her and not in God.

After the battle is recorded in Judges 4, a poem by Deborah is written in Judges 5 to show just how thankful she and Barak were for those who fought and to praise the Lord for his mercy in giving victory.

HEARING & LISTENING

One line in the Song of Deborah says, "The villagers ceased in Israel; they ceased to be until I arose; I, Deborah, arose as a mother in Israel" (Judg. 5:7). This description of Deborah shows just what role she predominately played in Israel—that of a mother. When we think of a mother, we think of someone who will hear our complaints and who seems to have all the answers we need to solve our problems. Deborah could listen to the problems of Israel, and with her wisdom make decisions on how they should best handle their situations. As mothers, don't we all wish we had the answers to all our questions? We wish we knew how to solve all the problems our children bring to us. But we do not always know the right words to say. How did Deborah come to have the knowledge to help all those people with their problems? She listened to the Lord.

In the time of the Judges and prophets, the Lord would communicate with those who had been appointed (e.g. Deborah). Then those individuals would relay that information to the Israelites who were listening. In Deut. 18:18, Moses says, "I will raise up for them a prophet like you from among their brothers. And I will put my words in his mouth, and he shall speak to them all that I command him." While Deborah had this special relationship with God, others who lived in Israel did not. They only heard from God through their prophets, judges, and priests. Today, we do not hear the physical voice of the Lord, but we do have something better—the Bible. The Bible, in all its verses and passages, can give us the answer to life's problems. We just have to listen to the words.

While all of life's pains can be healed and all its decisions be directed by the Bible, it may not address all of life's problems specifically. For instance, abortion is not mentioned in the Bible. There is not a verse that says, "Abortion is a sin" or "Thou shall not kill your unborn baby." However, there are many verses in the Bible that suggest that opting for abortion is a sin. Many times in both the Old and New Testament, the Lord gives an unborn child an identity and has a plan for their life. In Psa. 139:13-15, David writes, "For you formed my inward parts; you knitted me together in my mother's womb. I praise you, for I am fearfully and wonderfully made. Wonderful are your works; my soul knows it very well. My frame was not hidden from you, when I was being made in secret, intricately woven in the depths of the earth."

God knew what he was creating even deep inside a mother's womb. We can also look at the story of Elizabeth and see that the child in her womb leaped at the voice of Mary (Luke 1:41). We have two instances in which a baby has a purpose. We can infer, even from this early beginning of a separate life, that God had made a unique human being with a purpose, a plan, and the child was precious to the Lord. We also know that God said, "Do not kill." If God has created a unique human being, even inside a mother's womb, it is our responsibility to protect that life and not kill it. By studying these Scriptures and reflecting on God's will for creation, we can come to the conclusion that abortion is wrong.

However, the problems of life are greater than only the issue of abortion. We can know that God has given us all wisdom. In 2 Tim. 3:16, Paul writes, "All Scripture is breathed out by God and profitable for teaching, for reproof, for correction, and for training in righteousness." God has spoken to us today through his Word. He has given us the wisdom to learn from his words spoken thousands of years ago. More importantly, we can have confidence that if God directs our paths, then the wisdom he breathed through his Word will help us in all we do.

APPLYING HIS WORDS

We cannot just read the Scriptures; we have to interact with them. We have to read them, study the truths behind them, and apply them to our lives. If we want to become women of wisdom like Deborah and the treasured woman of Proverbs 31, we also have to listen to God. We have to understand his nature, teachings, and his desire for his creation—the desire that we all come to know him. The more we understand his words, the wiser we will become. The more we know his desire for our lives, the easier it will be to guide others in doing the right things. In fact, Solomon wrote, "The fear of the LORD is the beginning of wisdom, and the knowledge of the Holy One is insight" (Prov. 9:10).

When our children come to us wondering how they should handle certain situations, if we have God as our guide, then we can also guide our children in doing the right things. Not all the answers will easily appear before us, but we will have a starting point. Knowing that God can lead us into all wisdom can give us great comfort. Jesus said in John 16:13, "When the Spirit of truth comes, he will guide you into all the truth, for he will not speak on his own authority, but whatever he hears he will speak, and he will declare to you the things that are to come."

By applying God's wisdom to our own lives, we are less likely to encourage others to sin. Part of giving wise counsel to others is not only knowing what the right thing to do is, but also what they should not do. In 1 Pet. 2:8-9, the apostle wrote to many Christians in several different churches and encouraged them to stay strong in the Lord. "They stumble because they disobey the word, as they were destined to do. But you are a chosen race, a royal priesthood, a holy nation, a people for his own possession, that you may proclaim the excellencies of him who called you out of darkness into his marvelous light." When you know the word of the Lord and act upon it, you will not stumble!

SPREADING THE KNOWLEDGE

Throughout life, we will be faced with many tough decisions. People will come to us wanting to know the answers to difficult questions. We will need to be prepared. We will need someone to whom we can go and get sound advice. The amazing thing about Deborah is that she had the voice of the Lord guiding her in all she did. God whispered wisdom in her ear that she was able to relay to the people of Israel in sound judgments. Unfortunately, we do not have the voice of God whispering to us as we go throughout life. But we have the Bible. We also have a promise. God promises us that when we truly desire wisdom, he will grant it to us. "If any of you lacks wisdom, let him ask God, who gives generously to all without reproach, and it will be given him" (Jas. 1:5). If we truly desire to be women of wisdom, all we have to do is ask, and God will grant it.

Some of us see wisdom as a thing that eludes us. We think it may lie in fancy college degrees or that it comes from far off places or resides in distant cultures. In reality, wisdom is available to all who come before the Lord asking for it. God has given us his Word and his promise. Like Deborah and the treasured woman of Proverbs 31, we too can be women of wisdom. Deborah used it to help the Israelites, and the Proverbs 31 woman used it to manage her household. Once we have that wisdom, we have the responsibility to use it for God's glory.

DISCUSSION QUESTIONS:

1. How does God give us wisdom today?

2. God promised to grant us wisdom; how often do we pray for it?

3. Do we truly desire his wisdom, or justification for what we want?

4. How did Deborah relay her wisdom to the people of Israel?

5. How can we relay the wisdom and experience we have been given to those around us?

6. What verses in the Bible give us peace that God will guide us?

10

RAHAB

JOSHUA 2

She looks well to the ways of her household... – Prov. 31:27

The treasured woman is described as looking "well to the ways of her household." Out of all the descriptions of the Proverbs 31 woman, this characteristic seems to be the most overwhelming when you consider all the different directions our households may go every day. We could plague ourselves with questions like, *Am I feeding my family enough healthy foods or the right healthy foods? Are they dressed appropriately? Have I provided the right types of clothing and modest clothing? Am I scheduled enough? Am I too scheduled? Do I send my kids to school? Do I homeschool? Have I adequately prepared them to face the challenges of life?* On and on we could go. There is no end to the questions that could worry us concerning the health, safety, development, and spirituality of our children. But just as Jesus told Mary as she sat at his feet, "Only one thing is necessary," only one thing is truly necessary when raising our families. Do they have Christ at the center of their being, and do we have Christ at the center of our being?

In Scripture, it is a prostitute from a foreign land that shows us how to lead our family in being a God-centered people. Rahab was a prostitute in Jericho. Whether she chose this profession or it was forced on her by circumstances, we do not know. We do know she lived a sinful life far from the people of God. We also know from her story that once she had the opportunity to become a part of God's chosen race, she grabbed it. Rahab's story of becoming part of Israel is one filled with excitement and intrigue. And because of her faithfulness, she was blessed immensely—even becoming part of the lineage of Christ.

GRABBING ON TO GOD

When two spies sent by Joshua came to scope out the city of Jericho, they chose to stay at the home of Rahab. When a group of angry authorities came hunting the spies, she hid them on her roof. The people of Jericho knew of the Israelites. They knew Israel was the people of God and that God had guided them through battles in order to give them the land of Canaan. By the time the two spies reached Jericho, they had conquered two other cities and destroyed them. Knowing the Israelites were camped close by had caused much alarm in Jericho. The citizens were especially afraid when they discovered that two spies were prowling around. Rahab had also heard these stories. She knew of God's work and the loyalty of the Israelites to God's commands. She knew that God kept his word; if he meant to take Jericho for his people, then he would. Rahab did not want to be on the losing side in a battle against the Lord.

But how often do we choose to go against God? Some of us would rather our children play ball than praise the Lord. Others would rather spend money on things we do not need than spend it for God's glory. Some of us would rather read books or watch movies that go against God's will than spend time in the Word. Rahab knew the importance of having a relationship with God. She saw it in the lives of the Israelites. So often, we take our relationship with God for granted. Few of us have felt the urgency to turn to God like Rahab must have felt. There may not be Israelite warriors waiting at our city gates to conquer and destroy. God has freely offered us his love without the fear of imminent death hanging over us. Many of us do not cling to our faith as quickly as Rahab did, nor do we protect it as fiercely as she did. Nonetheless, Satan sits at the door of our hearts waiting for the opportunity to lead us into sin. Do we welcome him in?

PROTECTING THE FAITH

Once Rahab offered the spies refuge in her home, she hid them on her roof. She even lied to the authorities searching for them. And why did she protect them at the risk of her life? Because she knew she could trust God and that God would protect her family. She may not have had access to the Ten Commandments as the Israelites did. She had not witnessed first-hand the Exodus from Egypt or manna falling from the sky, but she had heard about this God. In Josh. 2:9-13, Rahab said, "I know that the LORD has given you the land, and that the fear of you has fallen upon us, and that all the inhabitants of the land melt away before you. For we have heard how the LORD dried up the water of the Red Sea before you when you came out of Egypt, and what you did to the two kings of the Amorites who were beyond the Jordan, to Sihon and Og, whom you devoted to destruction. And as soon as we heard it, our hearts melted, and there was no spirit left in any man because of you, for the LORD your God, he is God in the heavens above and on the earth beneath. Now then, please swear to me by the LORD that, as I have dealt kindly with you, you also will deal kindly with my father's house, and give me a sure sign that you will save alive my father and mother, my brothers and sisters, and all who belong to them, and deliver our lives from death."

As the two men were leaving, they promised protection for her family if she hung a red cord from her window. As long as she followed this command, she and her family would be saved from Jericho's impending doom. When given the choice of which way her family could go, Rahab chose God. She could have easily told the people of Jericho that there were spies hiding on her roof. She could have killed them as they lay there. She could have easily alerted others to the plans that the two spies had, but she did not. She chose God. She looked well to the ways of her family.

Looking well to the ways of our family means we should choose God and his will in everything that we do. When we are faced with matters of faith—and we all will be—are we faithful enough to know that God's way is always the best way? We must protect our faith and the faith of our children. Jesus told a parable in Matt. 13:45-46 about how precious our place in God's kingdom is worth. "Again, the kingdom of heaven is like a merchant in search of fine pearls, who, on finding one pearl of great value, went and sold all that he had and bought it." Is our faith that precious to us that we would give up everything else in order to keep believing? As daughters of the King and mothers of God's children, we must give up everything to do God's will!

HANGING OUR SCARLET CORDS

Rahab did not just protect the spies as they escaped from Jericho; she also followed their instructions. Before the impending attack, Rahab hung a scarlet cord from her window. As the city and everything in it was destroyed, Rahab and her family were safe in her home because of God's promise. Joshua 6:17 says, "And the city and all that is within it shall be devoted to the LORD for destruction. Only Rahab the prostitute and all who are with her in her house shall live, because she hid the messengers whom we sent." Very few of us are threatened physically because of what we believe. But our spiritual lives are constantly under attack. Like Rahab, our spiritual lives can be saved through obedience to the Father. Rahab simply had to hang a scarlet cord from her window, a sign that she believed and wanted to be a part of Israel. We too have a scarlet cord—baptism. Our baptism is an act of obedience signaling that we believe in Jesus and want to be part of God's family. Without this act of obedience, we never really join the family of God.

Being part of God's family is the most important thing we have to pass on to our children. Rahab chose God when she could have easily chosen other paths. She might have thought she could outsmart the Israelites and their God if she killed the spies or learned of their plans. We too might think we can figure it out on our own. If we just educate our children enough in the ways of the world, then they too can outsmart poverty or pain or struggles. But only the God of this world can give us what we truly need—a life in him. No matter what we do, we will struggle. Our struggles may all be different; they may be financial or physical. We may struggle with addiction or sin, with depression or laziness. But in the end, it will not be a book, a doctor, or a lot of money that will change our lives. It will be the overwhelming love of God and our desire to be with him.

LIVING WITH HIM

Committing our lives to the Lord will not necessarily mean we avoid all the pain of life. It does mean, however, that God will see us through. And just as God granted Rahab and her family a life with the Israelites because of her faith, God will grant us a life in heaven with him for eternity. Second Peter 3:13 promises us, "But according to his promise we are waiting for new heavens and a new earth in which righteousness dwells." As we look at the life of the Proverbs 31 woman, we see a treasured woman who glories God by guiding her household well.

Of the treasured woman, Proverbs says, "She looks well to the ways of her household and does not eat the bread of idleness" (31:27). The act of looking well to the ways of the household is not a passive position. It takes work and action; she does not eat the bread of idleness. Rahab worked to protect the lives of the spies and her family. She fought against things that would harm them in order to protect them, but ultimately, she fought to bring them closer to the true God. Rahab was a worthy opponent for the spiritual battle we all face. Do we fight like a warrior to protect our households? If we truly believe in the God of the Bible, how can we not do all we can to protect our families from the evils of the world and bring them closer to God? More than just their education, their physical well-being, or their emotional happiness, we should also be concerned with how closely we cling to the paths of the Lord. Rahab and the Proverbs 31 woman sought to bring their families as close to God as they could. In doing so, they showed the world how powerful God is. Do our actions and choices do the same?

DISCUSSION QUESTIONS:

1. What things distract us from the ways of the Lord?

2. How can we apply the ways of the Lord to other areas such as meal preparation, clothing, education, etc.?

3. What caused Rahab to have so much faith in the God of Israel?

4. Is fear a good reason for faith today?

5. How did Rahab protect her family?

6. How can we protect our faith?

7. Why was faith so precious to Rahab?

8. How can we make sure we protect our faith today?

11

HANNAH

1 SAMUEL 1:1-2:11

Her children rise up and call her blessed; her husband also, and he praises her. — Prov. 31:28

There is nothing worse than feeling betrayed by the people around you. When those who are supposed to support you instead make fun of you, belittle you, or ignore what you say or do, you are left with little confidence to go about your business, or you may even feel you have little value in the eyes of the Lord. It is in such a state that we find Hannah at the beginning of 1 Samuel. She is a woman clinging to what little hope she has—the grace and love of God.

In contrast, this is an image very unlike that of the Proverbs 31 woman. She is a woman from the beginning of the poem who is noted for her strength and confidence. We will find, however, that Hannah, despite all of her setbacks, is also strong in the Lord. She thus becomes a woman who can perform extraordinary acts of love. We too have strength in the Lord, a strength that can withstand many attacks. Paul writes in Eph. 6:10-11, "Finally, be strong in the Lord and in the strength of his might. Put on the whole armor of God, that you may be able to stand against the schemes of the devil." By standing with the Lord, we can resist all the forces that seem to tear us down. Children of the treasured woman rose up and called her blessed. Why? Because she had served her family well with the strength of the Lord.

STRANDED AND ALONE

Hannah was married to a man named Elkanah, who was also married to a woman named Peninnah. Though they were family, there was a lot of bitterness between the two wives. While Elkanah loved Hannah much more than he loved Peninnah, Hannah had no children and was convinced her womb was closed. Because Peninnah was jealous of Elkanah's affection, and Hannah had not borne any children, Peninnah teased Hannah until Hannah could not eat or sleep, and she did little but weep. And though Elkanah loved Hannah and gave her a double portion, he did not understand her pain or the reason for her despair. Even the priest, Eli, saw her as nothing more than a drunk woman. Hannah had no one to rely on except the Lord. Once Eli realized the depth of emotion Hannah was putting forth in her prayer, he was struck by her sincerity. He told her that her request would be granted by the Lord. Soon after the incident, Hannah became pregnant with her first son, Samuel.

We know from Scripture that Hannah's son became a great prophet of God, perhaps the most well-known in all the Old Testament. He was responsible for anointing the first two kings of Israel and guiding them in their decision-making. How was this sad and lonely woman so blessed to have a son so well-respected in Scripture? It's because she gave her son back to the Lord.

RETURNING OUR CHILDREN TO GOD

During Hannah's prayer, she made a promise to the Lord. In 1

Sam. 1:11, she prayed, "O LORD of hosts, if you will indeed look on the affliction of your servant and remember me and not forget your servant, but will give to your servant a son, then I will give him to the LORD all the days of his life, and no razor shall touch his head." Regardless of all the teasing Hannah endured and the anxiety she felt, she knew that the blessing the Lord would give her was not her own, but the Lord's. Hannah knew that if she were to conceive, the gift of a child would not be for her enjoyment, but a person who would grow up and need to know the Lord. Hannah's promise to the Lord was not empty. After only three years of life, Hannah took her precious son, Samuel, whom she prayed so diligently for, and gave him to Eli to be raised in the tabernacle. From then on, Hannah would see her son only once a year. She kept her promise to the Lord that Samuel would be his.

God gives us many blessings, from material possessions, talents, and abilities, to our precious children. Do we have the same strength that Hannah had to give our blessings back to the Lord? Do we use our talents for our enjoyment or to glorify God and bless his people? Do we have children for our pleasure or self-promotion, or do we raise them to be workers in the Kingdom?

Hannah could have kept her promised son at home. She could have paraded him in front of Peninnah each day and basked in the glory of getting back at her for the torment she had put Hannah through before Samuel's birth. But she did not. She gladly gave her son back to the Lord for his use. We too can keep what we have for our enjoyment and lose sight of the fact that God gave us that blessing, that talent, or that child for his glory. If we keep it hidden and never use it, then like the servant in the parable of the talents in Matt. 25:14-30, we will lose all we have without ever advancing the Kingdom of God.

COUNT YOUR BLESSINGS

We live in a material society. Often, we focus on what we do not have instead of the blessings God has piled upon us. The Proverbs 31 woman was called blessed by her children. Only a woman who realizes she is blessed and uses those blessings can convey that concept to her children. If we do not realize we are blessed, if we do not act like we live a life full of the blessings of God, then our children will never see us as a blessed woman.

Being blessed begins with the confidence that God is with us and has blessed us. If we want to use our blessings for the good of the Kingdom, we need to understand what blessings and abilities God has bestowed on us. Writing down all of our blessings is a good way to see the wonders God has given us. Once we've written down all our blessings, we should also write down how those blessing could be used in the Lord's work. For instance, those with young children should find ways to teach their children daily about God's love, promises, and mercy. Those with special skills like cooking, sewing, or teaching should find ways to use those talents in their church families. Those with time could use that blessing to teach others through Bible correspondence courses. There are many ways to work for the Lord. There are many programs and classes you can be a part of to help spread the gospel of Christ. The important thing is that we take what we have been given by God and give those things back to him through our service.

Often, we look to the church and wonder why it is not doing more to help those in need. We wonder why the church is not addressing all the problems plaguing our society (e.g. abortion, homosexuality, poverty). While there are many programs supported by the church to deal specifically with those issues, the heart of the matter is that it is not church leadership's responsibility, but ours. We are the church. If we are troubled that there is a growing need in our community that our church does not seem to be addressing, then we should not complain that our elders, preacher, or deacons are not doing their jobs. If we are taking the time to recognize a need and then complaining that it is not being met, are we not wasting time in helping those who are suffering?

It is our job to help the young girl who has found herself pregnant and alone. It is our job to reach out and to love sinners and try and show them a better way. It is our job to help the needy.

HER CHILDREN RISE UP...

When we use our abilities in service to the Kingdom, we will find that God has given us so much more than we thought. Those who see us working and using our talents will also recognize how blessed we are. When we sit at home feeling sorry for ourselves that we do not have this item, or that those around us make fun of us, then we are not working for the Lord or acknowledging his goodness. We must reach inside ourselves and decide that our talents and possessions are far greater than our sense of worthlessness. By working for the Father in spite of difficult circumstances, we can show to those around us how wonderful God is. The world will know that, despite our circumstances and insecurities, God is greater. He has given us blessings that matter in this world. How beautiful is it when a disabled person, who may seem to have so little on the outside, makes a great accomplishment in his life? How much more grand is it when a disabled person uses what she has for God? By using the talents God has given us, we glorify him.

Despite all that Hannah endured, she still established her hope on the promise that there was a God who loved her, had blessed her, and would continue to bless her. We too have that promise. Even when it seems God has forgotten us or has not blessed us, he has given us more than we can imagine. God loves us very much. He loves us so much that he gave us abilities, talents, and passions that we can use for his glory.

The treasured woman of Proverbs 31 is the ultimate worker for the Lord. Her work is why she is called blessed. She is not called blessed because she has wealth, beauty, or fame. She is called blessed because she has given all she has to her family and her Lord. True joy for us will not be realized when we have received all the material things we want in life. True joy will not come simply because we are surrounded by a lot of people. True joy and blessedness only come when we have given back to God and those around us. True joy comes when we take the beauty God has created within us and use it to glorify him.

DISCUSSION QUESTIONS:

1. How did Hannah feel at the beginning of her story?

2. How significant are her emotions to the promise she made to God?

3. When Hannah gave Samuel back to the Lord, what does she teach us about working for the Father?

4. What blessings do you have in your life?

5. How can you use them for the work of the church?

6. What programs do you have in your church or community that you could use your talents for?

7. The blessing of Hannah is that she gave back to the Lord and his service what she could have kept to herself. Are there things that we keep to ourselves that we can share more readily with others?

8. What blessing does the Proverbs 31 woman have and use for those around her that we can emulate?

12

ESTHER

ESTHER 1-10

Charm is deceitful, beauty is vain, but a woman who fears the Lord shall be praised. — Prov. 31:30

One of the greatest gifts God has bestowed upon women is beauty. He has given us the glory of our hair and physical attributes that attract men. It is a gift that we should honor and take care of much like our talents and abilities. However, we should never let our physical appearance outshine our spiritual development. Unfortunately, women throughout history have gone to great lengths to be beautiful. From make-up to diets to painful surgeries—there is no limit to what some women will do in order to convince the world of their beauty. But beauty always fails. Our beauty will not save us from the pains of life, nor will our beauty bring us closer to God. Eventually, our beauty will simply fade away. Fortunately, our fear and devotion to the Lord will keep us close to the Father as well as give us peace throughout all the turmoil of life. As we search the Scriptures, we see that the story of Esther is a good example of this truth. Although Esther was very beautiful, it was her faith in God and courage that saved an entire nation from death.

As daughters of the Most High, we too can have this courage, and we will find that the beauty of a deep and abiding faith in God is far greater than the beauty of our physical appearance.

CELEBRATING OUR BEAUTY

When we look at the entire passage of the Proverbs 31 woman, we do not see a woman so burdened by the tasks of life that her physical appearance no longer matters to her. In fact, the poet suggests in several lines that the Proverbs 31 woman has taken great care always to present herself to the world as well put together. She takes the time to make her arms strong, and she clothes herself in purple, an expensive and desired fabric of the time.

Obviously, she knows that her outward appearance is a representation of the beauty God has instilled inside of her. We are all representations of the Father. The image that we present to the world is a reflection of the person God made us to be. If that truth lives deep within us, should we not always seek to present our best? God made each of us a unique, beautiful individual. If we truly want others to know that we believe God created a wonderful person, should we not represent our Creator in the best way possible? Should we not dress in a way that pleases and honors God? If we want others to know that God is great and powerful, then we should take care of the beauty he has given us.

Knowing that our beauty is also a gift from the Lord does not mean that we should be wrapped up in our appearance. Our appearance is only part of who we are. God created us with so much more than just a beautiful appearance, he gave us talents, abilities, thoughts, and ideas. More importantly, he gave us his son. He created us to be his children and to have a relationship with him. The relationship we establish with the Father gives us hope, faith, and courage through difficult circumstances. Much like Esther in her dealings with the king, we see how Esther's faith and courage in the Lord, not her beauty, saved her.

BECOMING QUEEN

The story of Esther is an excitement-filled account of love, betrayal, and faith. The book begins with the ousting of the former queen, Vashti. Vashti is humiliated, and when asked to perform for the king, she refuses. Vashti's refusal leads to her banishment from the kingdom and the need for a new queen. The search for a new queen is not a simple process, but it is a competition of beauty and brains. Here we are first introduced to not only Esther, but her character. Esther is chosen as one of the beautiful virgins to be shown to the King as a possible replacement. For a year, Esther undergoes beauty treatments. In that year, Esther also gained favor with those who were in charge of the virgins to be brought before the king, specifically a man name Hegai. Because she had won favor, she was given special treatment. She got the best food and the best oils. She was given a position of honor among the virgins.

Despite all that she was given, Esther was not only obedient to those in charge, but she was also obedient to her family back home. Mordecai, Esther's uncle and guardian, had given her strict instructions to not reveal her heritage. Throughout the entire year of beauty treatments, Esther kept her mouth closed about who she was and from where she came. She also listened to Hegai. Before appearing before the king, Hegai gave her specific instructions to take only certain items with her. Because of her obedience and favor with Hegai, Esther became queen of the land. Esther did not get there simply by coincidence. With God's hand guiding her, Esther's preparations through her beauty treatments, her training, and her adherence to Mordecai and Hegai's instructions, Esther was primed to become the queen of the empire.

The Roman philosopher Seneca once said, "Luck is what happens when preparation meets opportunity." As Christians, we are constantly met with opportunities to spread God's word, to reflect his love, or to show his mercy. Had Esther not spent a year training herself and her body for judgment, she would not have been chosen. While God orchestrated the events in the account of Esther, Esther had to willingly and purposely comply. When we prepare ourselves both outwardly and inwardly to be an ambassador for God, we will meet the opportunities we have with the same success as Esther. All over the world, people are searching for God. They are desperate for the love and comfort he provides. In Acts 17:27, Paul was preaching to unbelievers on Mars Hill. He said, "that they should seek God, and perhaps feel their way toward him and find him." If we come into contact with someone desperate to seek God, hoping to feel something of his excellent nature, are we glorifying him in our appearance and actions?

But that wasn't the end of the story for Esther. Haman, the king's right-hand man, soon tricked the king into ordering the execution of all the Jews. Through a series of events, the fate of all Israel, God's chosen people, rested on the bravery and courage of Queen Esther. Esther can save her people by approaching the king. The king, however, has to approve Esther's visit. If he does not approve, then Esther could lose her life and fail to rescue God's children. Fortunately, the king did approve Esther's request and the nation was soon saved.

ESTHER'S EXAMPLE

While the story of Esther is intriguing and full of the providence of God, it is the example of Esther and her characteristics that can guide us to a more loving relationship with the Father. Throughout the account, Esther's actions always point back to an attitude of humility and devotion to her uncle and God, and using God's gifts for the good of the kingdom.

First, we see an attitude of humility in all that Esther does. Humility is not easily defined. Often, people think that humility is not thinking highly of yourself. Women, especially in strict religious cultures, often see humility as putting themselves down or not seeing themselves as valuable. However, humility does not mean a woman sees herself as worthless, but rather she understands her place in the kingdom. Esther knew no matter how powerful she became in the kingdom or how popular she became among the virgins, she still had a responsibility to do good works, to listen to Mordecai and Hegai, and rely upon God for his intervention. We all have the potential to be great and successful people. The greatness we possess, no matter the form—beauty, intelligence, or artisan—we owe that greatness to God. Without him, our existence would be meaningless, our potential hopeless, and our craft worthless. The arrogance that Esther could have obtained by her position in the kingdom could have been great. However, she still subjected herself to those who had helped and guided her. We are so blessed to be surrounded by a church family who can lead us through all the trials of life. Like Esther, we need to rely on them.

Second, Esther maintained her devotion to Mordecai and God. Part of being humble is knowing that you cannot be the person you are without the help and guidance of those around you. Esther understood this. She continued to listen to Mordecai even after becoming queen. She took into account the advice of Hegai instead of taking care of things herself. And when Esther was at her greatest need, not only did she ask for the prayers of her Israelite family, but spent time in prayer and fasting herself asking for the grace of God. We will face many challenges in life. Some of those challenges we think we will be able to handle ourselves. But through all of those challenges, we will have to have the guidance of the Father. Esther did not simply rely on herself though. She relied on the advice of those around her and the prayers of those who were also faithful. How many times do we think we can handle everything alone? How many times do we push others away that can help us in our journeys because we do not want to listen to their advice? How many times do we fail to pray in the simple decisions in our lives, then feel overwhelmed at trusting God in the big decisions? Just like the Proverbs 31 woman, Esther's humility and devotion caused her to be praised for centuries by the Israelite people. Both the Proverbs 31 woman and Esther's defining characteristic, more so than all the others they possess, is their devotion to the Lord. Can we say the same?

Third, Esther spent much of her time patiently preparing for the tasks that lay ahead of her. When she was preparing to go before the king the first time, she spent a year in beautifying her physical features. When she went to the king without permission, she waited a week—spending much time in prayer and fasting for the job that lay ahead of her. Once she gained the king's attention, she asked him twice to dine with her. She waited until the second time she dined with the king to lay before him her true heritage and Haman's betrayal. Esther prepared herself physically, spiritually, and mentally for what God placed before her. We read in Esth. 4:14 Mordecai's provocative question to Esther, "And who knows whether you have not come to the kingdom for such a time as this?" God did place Esther in the kingdom for this job. God also placed her there because she was well-equipped to handle the trials that this position offered. We do not know why God has placed us in certain positions. None of us can fathom the providence of God in our lives. He very well may have placed us in our times, in our homes, and in our jobs for a very specific purpose.

PREPARED FOR A PURPOSE

However, we have to take the time to prepare ourselves and our talents to be used by him. We live in an amazing time for women. We can be highly educated in whatever field we like. We can pursue careers in high positions or develop passions in whatever realm we choose. If we are truly devoted to God, then we will prepare and develop all the talents he has given us so that we can use them for his work. If we are not prepared to evangelize or teach, then we will not. If we have not prepared our talents that could help the needy, then we will not. If we have not prepared our minds to be completely devoted to him, then we won't. God cannot use the abilities we have not developed in our own lives, nor can we devote ourselves to him if we are only interested in living for ourselves. We must prepare ourselves to live for him.

God has given us incredible gifts—gifts of beauty, talents, and helpers. By using these gifts for God's glory, we will show the world God's greatness! By preparing the talents and gifts he has given us, we can do marvelous things for the Lord. We will also know how valuable we are in his sight. He gave us a unique, individualized work to do in his kingdom. Let's glorify him!

DISCUSSION QUESTIONS

1. Which quality of Esther do you admire most?

2. Do you view Esther as a beautiful woman who was blessed to become queen or a woman shaped by God? How does that translate to how you view yourself?

3. How did Esther rely on Mordecai and Hegai to help her become queen?

4. How can you better prepare your talents and gifts for the Lord?

5. Do you think God prepared you for a specific work in the kingdom?

6. How do you view humility?

7. How can you adopt a spirit of humility?

8. How can you rely on people in your spiritual family to help you develop your talents, abilities, and spiritual walk?

13

THE 21ST-CENTURY WOMAN

Give her of the fruit of her hands, and let her works praise her in the gates. – Prov. 31:31

The women of Scripture are beautiful, talented, and smart. And so are we. More importantly, the women of Scripture have a consuming faith. And so can we. It may very well seem impossible that the God of creation wants us to live and work for him, but he does. And just as the attributes of the Proverbs 31 woman may seem overwhelming and out of reach, they are not. The qualities exuded by the Proverbs 31 woman are not so unattainable that we cannot strive each day to achieve them.

Unfortunately, we live in a world full of excuses. We have excuses for why we can't go to school or work. We have excuses for our bad behavior. We even have excuses for why we can't be the woman God created us to be. However, we have no excuse that was not also available to the women of Scripture. They were normal women with the same aches and pains, trials and challenges, but they also yearned for God's love and blessings. They are like us in so many ways. Their example was preserved in Scripture so that we may learn from them and mimic their way of life.

SO WHAT DID WE LEARN?

The Proverbs 31 woman is the idealized woman fit to be the queen of Israel. Her attributes do not include a list of physical characteristics, but rather a list of works she engages in to please her family and God. While the list seems overwhelming, each task is done for the glory of her family and God. We may not accomplish everything the Proverbs 31 woman does physically, but we can adopt her lifestyle spiritually by prioritizing Christ above all. By doing that, we will become treasured like the Proverbs 31 woman.

Fortunately, we see this played out in the lives of the women of Scripture. So many of the obstacles we may face in choosing to put God first will seem to melt away.

For women who might ask, "What will others think of me if I devote all I am to God?" we can look to Mary, the mother of Jesus. Mary gave up her reputation and was willing to give up her husband to bear the Son of God.

Others might ask, "How can I give everything I have to others?" And we can look to Tabitha. She spent her days working for the good of widows and the poor. She not only gave to them; she honored them.

Some might say, "You don't know all I have lost and gone through! How can God expect anything of me?" And we can look to Ruth and her devotion. She lost her husband and the men who might have saved her from poverty. She even decided not to return to her parents in order to take care of Naomi. Ruth lost everything, but she still found something within herself to give to God.

Some might lament, "I have done too many bad things in my life for God to want me." And we can point them to Rahab the prostitute. She was a foreigner to God's people. She had nothing the Israelites wanted or envied. But she still believed in God and trusted in his promises.

Others might say, "My husband will never allow it!" We can tell them the story of Abigail. She was in a horrible marriage to a man who showed her no respect. She still chose to do the right thing, and God blessed her.

Still more will object, "You don't know how people treat me! How could God want me?" We can tell them about Hannah. Peninnah bullied her so badly that she could not eat or sleep. However, Hannah still praised and trusted in the Lord. When the opportunity came to get back at Peninnah, she did not. In fact, she used her son for the glory of God.

Some might even say, "I have nothing to give to God. Why would he want me?" We can then share the story of Esther, an orphan who only seemed to have a beautiful face. But once she started working for the good of God's people, she found that, with patience, she had a lot more to offer.

The lives of these women give us an example to imitate. God wants each of us. He wants us so much that he blessed us with ways to honor him so we could be assured of the promise to live with him eternally. What is holding us back from working for the Lord?

WHAT WE MUST DO

In order to be the woman God created us to be, we need first to decide that all we do will revolve around God. Each choice we make, each action we take, each word we speak must be a reflection of God reigning in our lives. With God at the heart of each action we take, we can truly proclaim the excellencies of the one who created us. Peter wrote, "But you are a chosen race, a royal priesthood, a holy nation, a people for his own possession, that you may proclaim the excellencies of him who called you out of darkness into his marvelous light" (1 Pet. 2:9). He was talking about you and me. Each of us has the power and ability to proclaim his greatness no matter what our talents and abilities are. For us to think otherwise is to doubt the greatness of our Father!

Making the decision to follow God completely can be an easy choice. It's the follow-through that is another matter. How can we stay faithful to God above when there are so many distractions in this world below? We should do as the women of Scripture did so long ago.

First, just as Mary chose to sit at Jesus' feet and listen to his words, we need to listen to the words of God. The world has many ideas on how we should live our life. It tells us how we should look and how we should think. The world tells us what it thinks is beautiful and what is right. But the world does not listen to God and his laws, and often the world will disagree. Like Mary, we need to shut the rest of the world out. If we want to stay faithful to God, we cannot entertain the ideas of the world. Mary chose the wise thing, rather than what was socially expected.

Second, like Priscilla, we need to continue to tell others about the love of God. By evangelizing, we will constantly remind ourselves of the grace God has shown us. If we want to remain faithful to the cause of Christ, and if we truly want to be a worker for him, then we must help others see the good things God has done. Priscilla stepped out of her community to go teach others the Gospel. She had to rely on God's guidance and help. Relying on God strengthens the bond we have with the Father. The more we rely on him, the less we can go about our business without him.

Third, like Lois and Eunice, our faith needs to be a part of our family. This mother and grandmother developed a sincere faith that could be passed down to Timothy. If we are trying to pass our faith down to our children, then we must have God at the center of all we do. With God as the constant focus and driving force of our lives, we will remain committed to him in all things.

Fourth, Rahab chose to be part of God's people. We too have to be part of the family of God. The encouragement we receive from other believers will help us remain in his care. Rahab walked away from all that was familiar so that she could be part of the community set apart from the rest of the world. When we enter the family of God, we too will be set apart from the rest of the world. The love and encouragement our church family can give us is much purer than the love offered by the world.

Fifth, like Hannah, we must bow in prayer. Prayer keeps us close to the Father. Through that communication with God, we will be reminded of his love, experience his grace, feel the comfort of his angels, and know that he will protect us.

Being God's woman may seem overwhelming. Emulating the Proverbs 31 woman may seem daunting. But God has given us many blessings so that we may achieve such a status. By studying the women of old, we can learn from both their triumphs and trials. We can know with certainty that we can work hard for the Lord, and in turn we will be blessed by the One who loves us so very much. With the help of God, the example of biblical women, the encouragement of other believers, and a strong desire to be close to the Father, we too can be a treasured woman—a Proverbs 31 woman.

DISCUSSION QUESTIONS:

1. What do you know about yourself in the presence of God?

2. Do you identify with one of the women of Scripture? If so which one?

3. Which woman in this study had the most impact on your walk with God?

4. What hinders you from having a closer relationship to the Father?

5. How can you be closer to the Lord?

CPSIA information can be obtained
at www.ICGtesting.com
Printed in the USA
FSOW03n1839250315
5941FS